LIFE WISH

LIFE WISH

REINCARNATION: REALITY OR HOAX?

MAURICE S. RAWLINGS, M.D.

THOMAS NELSON PUBLISHERS
Nashville • Camden • New York

Second printing

Copyright © 1981 by Maurice S. Rawlings

Published in Nashville, Tennessee, by Thomas
Nelson, Inc., Publishers and distributed in Canada
by Lawson Falle, Ltd., Cambridge, Ontario.

Printed in the United States of America.

Unless otherwise indicated, Scripture verses are
taken from the New American Standard Bible, © The
Lockman Foundation 1960, 1962, 1963, 1968, 1971,
1972, 1973, 1975, and are used by permission.

Library of Congress Cataloging in Publication Data

Rawlings, Maurice.
  Life wish.

  1. Christianity and reincarnation.   2. Rein-
carnation—Controversial literature.   I. Title.
BR115.R4R38   236'.2   81-16763
ISBN 0-8407-5792-1   AACR2

Mere living, what a profitless performance, mere painful living, what an absurd! . . . There is, then, nothing to be hoped for, nothing to be expected and nothing to be done save to await our turn to mount the scaffold and bid farewell to that colossal blunder, the much-ado-about-nothing world . . .

It is the thought that death appears to proclaim, the thought of frustration and final unreason at the heart of things, that is itself the root of the pessimist's despair . . . Give assurance that it is not so, and the scene is changed. The sky brightens, the door is left open for unimagined possibilities, things begin to fall into an intelligible pattern. . . .

> —W. Macneile Dixon in *The Human Situation*
> Gifford Lectures at the University of Glasgow
> 1936–37

But thanks be to God, who gives us the victory through our Lord Jesus Christ.

> —1 Corinthians 15:57

CONTENTS

Acknowledgments

The idea for this book arose from some strange encounters I had while traveling for the American Heart Association and during promotional tours for my previous books. Since I am not an expert in Eastern religions—nor in any religion, for that matter—the data I found required considerable organization and interpretation.

Restructuring of the material came from the untiring efforts of my editor, Peter Gillquist, of Thomas Nelson Publishers. Interpretation was monitored by the skills of Bob and Gretchen Passantino of Santa Ana, California. The fine library and Information and Referral Service of the Spiritual Counterfeits Project, Berkeley, California, provided materials unavailable elsewhere, along with the expertise of Virginia Hearn and her staff.

Grammatical and stylistic corrections were made through the kindness of Dr. Bert Bach, Dean of Faculty, the University of Tennessee at Chattanooga. Indirect assistance came through Rev. Matthew McGowan of Central Presbyterian Church, Kay Arthur of Reach Out, Inc., Rev. Ben Haden of First Presbyterian Church, Dr. Lexie Wiggins, Assistant Dean of Tennessee Temple University, and Spencer McCallie, Jr., of McCallie School in Chattanooga.

The remarkable capabilities of my secretary at the Diagnostic Center, Joan Burnett, undergirded many re-typings of the manuscript. She often gave me the encouragement I needed.

Without these people and the forbearance of my family and my fellow-physicians, this book could not have been completed.

Foreword

Today we live in a vast marketplace. Someone is always selling something to somebody somewhere. Wherever we turn, we are being enticed to buy: products, merchandise, ideas, organizations.

Even religion seems to be for sale. All around us people proclaim their own religious ideas as the best, greatest, most spiritual—all guaranteed to satisfy the spiritual craving deep within each of us.

The "new world religions" are making a special offer: reincarnation. Reincarnation is the best-selling feature of many of today's popular religions. But God holds out another offer: salvation and resurrection. Which offer is better? Or is it important that we make a choice at all?

Between the two mysteries of life—birth and death— comes yet another mystery: the purpose of life. What are we here for? Do we exist to satisfy our innate cravings and basic drives? Or is the purpose of life to honor and love a Creator for creating us? Were we created and placed here with accountability to Someone? Or did we just "get here," miraculously evolving from prehistoric nothingness and responsible to no one?

Is life intended to prepare us for death? Or should the purpose of life be to prepare for yet another life?

And death—how do we find out about that? Is there more to death than oblivion? Is death *the* end? If there is more, are we repeatedly recycled into a predetermined new life in this world, or do we enter an unseen dimension of this or another world? Do we enter a spirit world existent long before our own conception, where we join our Creator—a spirit world containing the realms of heaven and hell?

As a physician who observes the mysteries of birth and death daily, I have become convinced that certain stages in the life process partially unveil these mysteries of our existence.

As children, we normally possess a certain zest for living, along with an intense desire to gratify our own needs. In adulthood, life's burning questions become boring and irrelevant. Most of us concentrate only on survival and daily living. Only when death looms imminent do we search desperately for some meaning beyond the often unrewarding existence we see around us.

How many of us discover that life's purpose has eluded us because of our own negligence? In our waning years, the existential search becomes a desperate attempt to satisfy this life-void, this unfulfilled yearning of the soul.

Religion deals with life (or nonlife) after death. To answer my own questions about death, I turned to the sacred writings of many faiths to try to find answers. When I began to see how they conflicted in their claims, I tried to correlate those writings with the reports of my patients who had been retrieved from death—people who claim to have "been there."

Several patients came back to life with amazing reports, some of which offer enlightenment to this dilemma of what happens after death. Those reports formed the basis of my first two books, *Beyond Death's Door* and *Before Death Comes*.

In this book, I present new data, based in part on the experiences of these patients, concerning the subject of reincarnation, comparing it with the claims of Christianity and other religions. Reincarnation is a *life* wish; hence the name of the book. But is it more than just a wish?

After research into many faiths and many bibles, I now know that only one ancient Book holds the answer to these mysteries. While comparing my patients' experiences to what the Bible says about heaven or hell, I thought to myself, *Just suppose the Bible is true, word for word, and not merely a history book with a few embellishments.* That unnerving thought was followed by another: *If the Bible is true, then why do many of my Christian friends try to "update" its truth with popular versions of reincarnation?*

This book is my attempt to answer such questions.

CHAPTER 1

HERE TODAY AND BACK TOMORROW

Belief in *reincarnation* is flourishing in America. The word means "to come back into flesh." Reincarnationists believe that each soul survives after death and then is reborn into the body of another human being.

Until recently, serious belief in reincarnation in the Western world was confined largely to spiritualist and occult groups or to individuals influenced by the writings of such groups. Yet over the centuries, countless poets, writers, and philosophers, as well as some scientists, have made statements reflecting their personal attraction to the possibility of reincarnation.

Today the spread of Eastern religions into the West has popularized the concept of reincarnation to an extent unimaginable even twenty years ago. Celebrities as well as ordinary people discuss the subject with an offhandedness that shows how extensively and uncritically the idea is being accepted. In what other context could Olivia Hussey (who played Jesus' mother in Franco Zeffirelli's *Jesus of Nazareth*) casually explain to a film critic that she was right for the part of Mary because she was, in fact, the reincarnation of Mary, the mother of Jesus? Some form of reincarnation now seems almost taken for granted as the most acceptable explanation of what happens after death.

True Believers?

For some reason, stories about famous people's belief in reincarnation intrigue us most, though few of us would give much credence to the accounts we see headlined in supermarket tabloid newspapers. Here are a few of the better-documented stories about what some famous persons have said on the subject of reincarnation.

General George S. Patton. The 1980s have brought a powerful 1970 film, *Patton*, back to TV and movie screens. General George S. Patton (1885–1945), an Allied general in World War II, commanded forces in North Africa, in Sicily, and in the invasion of Europe that led to Hitler's defeat. Although privately wealthy, Patton stayed in the military because he loved wars and fighting. He was labeled "Blood and Guts" Patton by wartime reporters because of his recklessness and daring in combat. (Men fighting under him, however, are said to have commented, "Yeah, *our* blood and *his* guts!")[1] Many sources report that Patton believed in reincarnation.

The magazine *California Today*, part of the San Jose *Mercury News*, said that "Gen. George Patton thought he was an incarnation of one of Napoleon's generals and claimed to be able to recall intricate details of battles once fought and long forgotten. None of this would have surprised Napoleon, who frequently declared himself to be Charlemagne reborn."

In his 1979 book for junior high students, I. G. Edmonds added more details to that legend. He described Patton as believing that:

---

[1] I. G. Edmonds, *Other Lives: The Story of Reincarnation* (New York: McGraw-Hill, 1979), p. 5.

he had once fought as a legion commander in Caesar's army. He was sure he had been there when the Greeks built the great Trojan horse that led to the fall of Troy. He also—if you believe him—fought beside Richard the Lion-Hearted in the Third Crusade (A.D. 1189–1199) to free the Holy Land from the Saracens.

Patton was equally certain that he would go on fighting wars in future lives as he had in past ones. He made this clear in a poem he wrote. One line of the poem reads, "So forever in the future, shall I battle as of yore."[2]

Loretta Lynn. In the 1977 book, *Coal Miner's Daughter*, which was later made into a movie, country singer Loretta Lynn (b. 1935) described a trance-like vision she once had. "I know *I've* got ESP. . . . I believe in reincarnation, too. . . . I was an Indian woman wearing moccasins and a long buckskin dress and I had my hair in pigtails." Her husband was the chief. In another experience she "saw herself" dressed in an Irish costume. "I know my church doesn't believe in reincarnation, but sometimes I'm positive I was really an Indian and an Irish girl in times before this one.[3]

Carl Gustav Jung. Carl Gustav Jung (1875–1961) was a Swiss psychiatrist who departed from the sex-oriented views of Sigmund Freud to develop his own school of psychology. Jung was especially interested in what could be learned about human personality from studying primitive mythology. "Rebirth," he said, [in its various forms of reincarnation, resurrection, and transformation] "is an affirmation that must be counted among the primordial affirmations of mankind."[4] Although he never

---

[2]Ibid.

[3]Loretta Lynn and George Vessey, *Loretta Lynn: Coal Miner's Daughter* (New York: Warner Books, 1977), pp. 68,69.

[4]As quoted in Joseph Head and S. L. Cranston, *Reincarnation: The Phoenix Fire Mystery* (New York: Julian Press/Crown Publishers, Inc., 1977), p. 187.

declared himself convinced of reincarnation (for lack of empirical evidence), his lectures and other writings reveal his interest in the question:

My life as I lived it had often seemed to me like a story that has no beginning and no end. I had the feeling that I was a historical fragment, an excerpt for which the preceding and succeeding text was missing. . . . I could well imagine that I might have lived in former centuries and there encountered questions I was not yet able to answer; that I had to be born again because I had not fulfilled the task that was given to me. When I die, my deeds will follow along with me—that is how I imagine it. I will bring with me what I have done. In the meantime it is important to insure that I do not stand at the end with empty hands. . . .[5]

Henry Ford. Mass production of automobiles was first developed by Henry Ford (1863–1947). His use of the conveyor belt and factory assembly line enabled cars to be produced in large quantity and therefore cheaply.[6] Ford was a member of the Theosophical Society and a firm believer in reincarnation. A 1928 interview in the San Francisco *Examiner* quoted him as follows:

I adopted the theory of Reincarnation when I was twenty-six. . . . Work is futile if we cannot utilize the experience we collect in one life in the next. When I discovered Reincarnation it was as if I had found a universal plan. I realized that there was a chance to work out my ideas. Time was no longer limited. I was no longer a slave to the hands of the clock. . . . Some seem to think [genius] is a gift or talent, but it is the fruit of long experience in many lives. Some are older souls than others, and so they know more.[7]

---

[5]From Jung's posthumous autobiography, *Memories, Dreams, Reflections* (New York: Pantheon, 1963), as quoted in Head and Cranston, 1977, p. 447.

[6]Edmonds, p. 4.

[7]As quoted in Joseph Head and S. L. Cranston, *Reincarnation: An East-West Anthology* (Wheaton, Ill.: The Theosophical Publishing House, 1961), pp. 270,271.

Past-Lives Therapy

Interest in reincarnation in this country is in many ways a grass-roots movement. A few public figures like Dick Cavett, Merv Griffin, and Doug Henning have been vocal about their devotion to Transcendental Meditation, but more than a million people in the U.S. are now said to practice that technique. Undoubtedly, some of those people have adopted at least part of TM's teaching about reincarnation. It comes as no surprise that hypnotists, workshop leaders, psychologists, and therapists of all sorts have climbed aboard the reincarnation bandwagon.

Celebrities like George Hamilton, Phyllis Diller, Mac Davis, Lola Falana, Lee Majors, Sean Connery, and others have been featured in stories about supposed past-life experiences that were revealed under hypnotic regression. Thousands of everyday people, too, take part in past-lives therapy, trying to understand the problems of their present life by pinpointing the traumas of supposed previous existences.

In an objective, carefully researched article in a popular magazine, one writer commented: It seems that "anyone instructed by a hypnotist to return to a previous life will find something to report."[8] That article noted that a San Francisco psychologist, after doing seven hundred fifty past-life recalls with clients, reported that most of those individuals described mere peasant existences rather than coming up with well-known historical figures as the persons they once were.

The foremost academic investigator of human survival after death is Ian Stevenson (b. 1918). A professor of

---

[8]Kenneth L. Woodward, "Do We Live More Than Once?" *McCall's* 106:28 (June 1979), p. 128.

psychiatry at the University of Virginia School of Medicine, Stevenson has been a pioneer in applying "modern methods of recording, verification and analysis" to cases of supposed reincarnation. Until he did so, "incidents of alleged rebirth remained in the categories of legend, folklore, and unsupported claims."[9] Stevenson tends to be suspicious of any information uncovered during hypnosis. He regards nearly all such accounts as entirely imaginary, "because one cannot control the subconscious influences derived from information to which the adults have been exposed."[10] Stevenson's own research focused primarily on very young children and what they seemed to recall about past lives. In a 1960 essay, Stevenson said: "The evidence I have assembled and reviewed here does not warrant any firm conclusion about reincarnation. But it does justify, I believe, a much more extensive and more sympathetic study of this hypothesis than it has hitherto received in the West."[11]

In *Twenty Cases Suggestive of Reincarnation*, which was first published in 1966, Stevenson described persons he had investigated firsthand:

The "personalities" usually evoked during hypnotically-induced regressions to a "previous life" seem to comprise a mixture of . . . the subject's current personality, his expectations of what he thinks the hypnotist wants, his fantasies of what he thinks his previous life ought to have been, and also perhaps elements derived paranormally. . . .

---

[9]Helen McCarthy, "From the Files of Dr. Ian Stevenson," in Martin Ebon, ed., *Reincarnation in the Twentieth Century* (New York: World Publishing Co., 1969), p. 113.

[10]Woodward, p. 132. The ability of the subconscious mind to record data ignored or soon forgotten by the conscious mind is called *cryptomnesia* (Craig R. Waters, "You Are There: Past Lives Therapy," *New Times* 10, Feb. 20, 1978, p. 58).

[11]As quoted in Head and Cranston, 1977, pp. 434.

I believe . . . that the evidence favoring reincarnation as a hypothesis for cases of this type [those that he had investigated] has increased. . . .[12]

This professor is clearly open to considering reincarnation a valid experience, although he continues to state that he has "proved" nothing. In the foreword to his 1974 revision of *Twenty Cases*, he again stressed this fact:

I would here only reiterate that I consider these cases *suggestive* of reincarnation and nothing more. All the cases have deficiencies as have all their reports. Neither any case individually nor all of them collectively offers anything like a proof of reincarnation. My most important single conclusion about them is of the need for further study of similar cases. If anyone takes up this task I shall consider my efforts amply rewarded.[13]

Stevenson has since written five more books about his continuing research.[14] *Xenoglossy* (1974) is an extensive study of an American woman who spoke Swedish under hypnosis. After a lengthy discussion of the possibilities of fraud, cryptesthesia, and "super-ESP" as explanations, Stevenson states that, rather than hypothesizing reincarnation in that case, he tended to regard *possession* (defined as the influence of a discarnate personality) as "slightly more suitable as the correct interpretation" (p. 84).

---

[12]Ibid., p. 436.

[13]Ian Stevenson, M.D., *Twenty Cases Suggestive of Reincarnation* (Charlottesville: University Press of Virginia, 1974), p. x.

[14]These books are *Cases of the Reincarnation Type* (Volume I: *Ten Cases in India;* Volume II: *Ten Cases in Sri Lanka;* Volume III: *Ten Cases in Lebanon and Turkey*), *Xenoglossy: A Review and Report of a Case*, and *Telepathic Impressions: A Review and Report of Thirty-Five New Cases*. All are published by the University Press of Virginia.

The Lion Lady

I became acquainted with the popularity of reincarnation quite by accident. . .

"Now remember, you promised not to laugh if I told you this, so here goes. Although you'd never guess it, I was actually a lion in my previous life. A ferocious, huge, man-eating lion. I had a beautiful long reddish mane, and I lived way out in the plains of South Africa. I was under the law of the jungle: kill or be killed.

"One day I remember being stalked by a white hunter on a large safari. Before I heard them, I felt the bullets from his high-powered rifle as they slammed into my side. Just after I was hit I recall how my majestic mane became bloodstained as it dragged the ground. My front legs were paralyzed and useless, so I kept pushing myself forward with my hind legs, getting blood all over my mane. I still had the instinct to survive. By that time I knew I was dying and I remember asking myself over and over, 'Why did I deserve this? What did I do wrong?' "

The woman speaking wasn't talking to me. She was telling this story to the person sitting just in front of me in an unlit area of a TV studio. She did indeed, I marveled, have unruly red hair. It was spilling down her back in long curls like a regal mane. *What a coincidence,* I thought, *she really resembles a lion.* I also noticed that her long pointed red fingernails reflected the floodlights on the far side of three TV cameras. The lights outlined several crew members lounging and waiting to tape the next segment of the daily talk show. I wondered if the director and producer might not be more interested in the unrehearsed scenario now going on in front of me than in their planned program.

The red-haired lion lady was on the set to promote a book for the professional advertising agency she represented. During a lull in the conversation I asked her a question. She disengaged herself from her conversation with her client, the author of the book, to turn around to look at me. Sure enough, she had big brown eyes.

"No, he's not my husband," she answered. "I arrange his TV and radio shows. We're promoting his book, which is about real estate and how to make money without paying taxes. It's selling real well."

As we continued talking, I couldn't help being amused. She really did look like a lion. She had even dressed the part, with a thick hairy brown sweater, curious red shoes, and a wild array of oversized jewelry.

When she found out that I was promoting a book about accounts of life after death, she said, "Let me tell you more about my other past lives, the lives I've lived since being a lion." Of course I was curious.

"You probably won't believe this," she continued, "but my former husband and I both became aware one day that we actually had known each other in a previous life. In fact we had lived together in a previous marriage. We actually recognized each other intimately. But it was a strange recognition. Our roles were reversed in the former marriage. I was the husband, and he was the wife. Perhaps that's why we didn't get along as well this time. I don't know the reason, but we fared better when our sexes were reversed.

"There's no doubt at all that we knew each other before. We could recall the same relatives as well as the same events. That first marriage occurred three generations before the second one.

"We've been able to research the facts and have documented a lot of this. When we were able to find the stores and hotels we recalled and to trace the people that existed at that time, each of us was surprised. Sounds crazy, doesn't it? But it's true. And I have other lives I can recall too. After our segment on camera is completed, I'll tell you about some of them. I think we're up next."

I was bewildered. I didn't know what to say. I had encountered other people who claimed previous lives, but none quite this bizarre. This case involved animals, and most of the others seemed limited to humans.

When the red-haired lion lady and her companion finished their appearance, the stage crews began rearranging the set for me. The tax-dodging real estate professional spoke up as I approached. She had told him I was interested in reincarnation.

"I've had previous lives also," he said. "I've seen places that I recognized from many centuries ago. Dorothy here [he was pointing to his agent] has been a great help to me in analyzing these events. They are really fascinating, and we've been able to verify many of the instances."

"By the way," he continued, "have *you* had any experiences of *déjà vu*—feeling like you've been someplace before or recognizing something you've seen before? If you have, then you should make it a point to get better acquainted with Dorothy. She's helped many people to find their past lives. I'm sure she can help you too."

I wasn't about to get better acquainted with Dorothy. I had problems enough of my own—problems concerning people's beliefs. Everybody believes in something. I wanted to understand what motivates people to reach the religious conclusions they do.

Reincarnation Is "In"

Death is the great leveler, the most democratic of processes. Every human being, every living thing, participates in it. So in that crazy world of cameras and studios I became even more interested in what people believe about an afterlife and about themselves. I knew that belief in reincarnation was common, especially among Hollywood and other show business personalities. Many of these individuals present convincing data, and their beliefs are often adopted, or at least tolerated, by people in general.

The spread of Far Eastern religions into the West has popularized the concept of reincarnation. The press and TV media likewise find the allied areas of parapsychology fascinating to the American public. It makes good copy.

I recall an incident in Louisville, Kentucky. I was interviewed by a newspaper editor who allowed me to interview him in return. He estimated that, historically, over half the human race had accepted the concept of reincarnation at one time or another.

"After all," he said, "reincarnation is the most comforting of all beliefs about the afterlife. There is no doubt in my mind that I have had previous lifetimes. For instance, I was a Shakespearean actor in England in one life. You can probably recall some of your own.

"I also believe that civilizations have recycled for eons of time, surviving many previous atomic wars. We merely rediscovered the atomic bomb in our present lifetime. It wasn't new at all. After each atomic holocaust a few apelike creatures were probably left, with their memory recall serving to restructure the next civilization."

I asked this editor about the beliefs of Hindus, Buddhists, and followers of other Far Eastern faiths.

"I believe we all come back in our own kind—an animal as an animal and a human as a human," he said. This, he emphasized, was the popular version of reincarnation in the West. *Transmigration* (reincarnation in the form of another species) is popular only in the East.

He declined to discuss eternity, stating that it was far beyond his conception—too frightening to think about. He couldn't accept the idea of heaven or hell either, because he didn't want to stay in one place that long. "I want to come back to this world. I love life, and I don't want to lose it. That's why reincarnation appeals to me.

"Think of it this way. Death allows the seed of the soul to float out into the air, and the seed somehow comes to rest in the womb of a female where it eventually combines with a sperm as the third seed. And there you are! You are back, ready to be born again in this life as another individual. You are home free."

A New Religious Outlook

I began talking with more and more people about life after death. The details of their beliefs changed but often there was that common denominator: reincarnation. I was beginning to see for myself that reincarnation was the "in" thing today in lots of people's lives, even among Christians.

Why has reincarnation become so popular? People believe in reincarnation because it seems like a comfortable, logical answer to the problem of sin and God's acceptance. It is reassuring to think that if you mess up in this life, you have hundreds of more lives ahead in which to straighten things out. Salvation can be yours!

All you have to do is get through the next few hundred lives, burning off your sins until you are perfect. As I was told by one college student at UCLA, "Who wants eternity elsewhere, when I can have another life in a world with which I am already familiar? I don't want the purgatory that you Christians sell. I want life and I want it now—right here, and I want it in the next life also. I want the best of everything. So you see, I don't want you to convert me—I want to convert you."

(Other people have tried to convert me to reincarnation by way of letters. The subject of life after death makes fascinating conversation everywhere, for everyone seems to have an opinion!)

But there is more behind this current openness to reincarnation teaching. People today want a meaningful religious experience *now*. Instead of emphasizing the *past* (when God supposedly did marvelous things) and the *future* (when God's promises supposedly will be fulfilled), they say they want something in the *present*. Regrettably, few churches seem to provide any compelling appeal to that yearning for present meaningfulness. The spiritual poverty permitted by many contemporary established religions has encouraged men and women to opt for new experimental religions that encourage feelings and self-expression. Why does the church seem irrelevant to so many people's current needs and questions? The problem is complex.

And so, the void of the church's ineffective witness is being filled by a new religious outlook. The East and West coasts serve as mixing bowls where the forces of the occult strengthen the religions of the Far East. Traditions and moral standards on which America was founded are being discarded. In the year 1638, only eighteen years after the Pilgrims set foot on Plymouth Rock, the Puritans established what is now Harvard

University. An official guideline for students stated: "Everyone shall consider the main end of his life and studies to know God and Jesus Christ which is eternal life." In talking to some Harvard students, I discovered that their guideline now is the atheism of Karl Marx or Lenin or some exotic Eastern faith.

Values have changed. At one time both our universities and our currency were based on a Christian concept, "In God We Trust." Yet a 1978 Gallup Poll showed that only nineteen percent of the nation attended Bible study groups, while twenty-five percent practiced transcendental meditation. Twenty-five percent stated they "almost never" attended religious services, although eighty-nine percent of that number thought they still believed in God or a "universal spirit."[15] Religions that are characterized by feelings instead of faith are displacing Christianity for the world's younger inhabitants.

The turbulent social conditions of the 1960s may have allowed these new religions to multiply more rapidly. During that decade and since then, disillusionment has grown among the young to an extent that seems unmatched in history. President Kennedy was gunned down in Dallas, the Beatles introduced a musical revolution, Harvard professor Timothy Leary introduced LSD as a substitute for religion, and the Supreme Court outlawed prayer in public schools. We lost the war on poverty about the time we lost the war in Viet Nam. The civil rights movement faltered when Martin Luther King, Jr., was martyred. The militant Black Muslim movement started to flourish. The government was found to be undeniably corrupt with the Watergate fiasco. Drug use became widespread. Inflation and crime

---

[15]George H. Gallup, *The Gallup Poll, 1978* (Wilmington: S. R. Scholarly Resources, Inc., 1978), pp. 76,77,637.

skyrocketed. Abortions were legalized, and contempt for Christian principles and family structures became evident everywhere. Crumbling traditions encouraged experimentation with new religions.

In a time of upheaval and insecurity, proponents of teachings that incorporate reincarnation have an easy time getting people to subscribe to their philosophies. The wife of one of my colleagues is now innocently teaching yoga in the public schools as a form of exercise for physical fitness. A minister in our city practices transcendental meditation for "relaxation of the emotions." He does not feel that it interferes with his Christian faith but rather augments it. Two of several doctors I know who practice hypnosis with their patients eventually tried it themselves. They turned to self-hypnosis to get rid of the smoking habit and "to improve the mind." Now both are experimenting with meditation, using "cosmic forces" to "soul-travel."

Many people follow daily horoscopes to determine travel plans, business ventures, and personal decisions, large or small. Even Christians "ask the stars." (Why not ask Jesus Christ who put the stars there in the first place [see Jer. 10:12]?)

In larger cities, parapsychologists are experiencing thriving practices. I contacted one who is investigating near-death experiences among patients (he is renowned for his research in extrasensory perception—ESP). Since he was an expert in dealing with the supernatural or spirit world, I asked him if he had encountered any good or evil forces in this world. His reply was not what I expected: "We parapsychologists believe in the supernatural as a neutral force. We don't believe in Satan or evil powers, so why would we believe in God? We believe that ESP is a natural phenomenon under human control and of human origin."

Continuing the conversation, I asked, "If the supernatural is under human control, what does the Bible mean when it says 'That which is born of the flesh is flesh, and that which is born of the Spirit is spirit'?" (John 3:6). He replied that he didn't believe in the Bible. He was a scientist and therefore an agnostic; he seemed to equate the two.

It would be comforting to dismiss those examples as nothing more than people caught up in a passing cultural fad. But I believe they are symptomatic of something far more urgent. Recently we have witnessed an explosion of new cults and sects unlike anything in history. Most of these new cults are based on reincarnation. They are Westernized blends of the ancient Eastern faiths of Hinduism and Buddhism, the occult lore of Egypt and Babylon, and refinements of Greek philosophical speculations.

Clearly, a new religious outlook is sweeping America today. Although it sometimes hides under the guise of science, it has its base in a religious urge, a *life wish* for existence beyond the grave.

Why Reincarnation?

Reincarnation is a man-made solution to the problems of evil, disease, catastrophe, and injustice. Basic to Hinduism is its presupposition of the retributive justice of the universe. If the universe somehow "takes account of" the good and bad actions of each person's life, and if there is no sacrifice for wrongdoing, then each person must pay for his or her own sins. That is the inexorable law called *karma* in Hinduism, and reincarnation seems to be a plausible way out.

In Eastern thought, *all* action is regarded as a kind of sin. Cyclical rebirth is considered necessary, since it is almost impossible for a person to make up for all of his or her sins in one lifetime. Instead, the argument goes, one must be reborn at a station in life commensurate with the good and bad deeds of one's previous life. In the traditional Eastern view, the soul will eventually balance out all deeds, good *and* bad, from all past lives and in that way will be liberated from the cycle of death and rebirth. The rebirth cycle is considered the result of karma, the force generated by one's actions in previous lives that empowers the continuance of the cycle. The goal is to become "enlightened," which is achieved through a discipline of meditation, yoga, and elimination of natural desires. Hopefully, with each successive life, the soul will come closer to enlightenment and eventually break the rebirth cycle.

The original Hindu concept is different from the way reincarnation is understood by Westerners today. Because of the influence of Christianity in our culture, people tend to think of reincarnation as an opportunity to atone for sins. They see it as a chance to accumulate more good deeds than bad deeds, and so end up a good person after all. Such a view, however, is not a proper understanding of the Hindu law of karma. The salvation of Eastern thought is a salvation of having to undo all works, good or bad.

In Eastern thought, reincarnation becomes the obvious explanation for the inequities we see in the world around us. Is it fair for an innocent baby to be born in poverty? It is, if that poverty is retributive punishment for that soul's greedy action in a previous life. Is it fair for a seemingly good man to suffer the horrors of cancer? It is, if he abused his wife and children in a previous life. Is it fair for a bad man to prosper? It is, if we know that karmic law is giving him what he deserves. Is it fair for a tyrant to live into his nineties? It is, if we know that in his next life he will suffer for his tyranny. Reincarnation provides an answer to the tough question of the world's inequitable treatment of individuals—and also gives the reason we should not interfere.

Reincarnation in History

Reincarnation is a very old idea. It has always been a prominent and integral part of almost all Eastern religions. As Hinduism, the mother of Eastern thought, developed over the last four thousand years, karmic law and reincarnation were two of its basic tenets. Most of its offshoots still retain that emphasis. Modern Eastern imports—yoga sects and theosophy in particular—emphasize the importance of karma and reincarnation.

The terms *reincarnation* and *transmigration* can be used interchangeably. But I will use the term reincarnation to refer to the view that humans always return as humans, reserving transmigration for the belief that one species or life form can return in another form. That is, one can be reborn as a human being, an animal, even an insect; some even believe that one can be reborn as an inanimate object, such as a rock. The lion lady in the TV studio accepted transmigration. In general, however, transmigration is not very popular with Western reincarnationists. After all, who wants to come back as a worm?

Reincarnation is not new to Western thought. As early as 550 B.C. the Greek philosopher and mathematician Pythagoras proposed a theory of transmigration, which included reincarnation. He taught that the ideal existence is a life of divine bliss attained after final escape from a cycle of intermediate rebirths.

That final state of salvation was reached only through purification, renunciation of worldly sensuality, and observance of ascetic abstinence. Intellectual activity was considered the noblest form of purification. Pythagoras even had his own brand of karmic law, stating that the moral quality of one's present life determined the nature of the body which the soul would inhabit in the next life.

Greek thought had considerable influence on a few early Christian theologians, especially those like Clement of Alexandria (A.D. 155–220), who operated on the fringes of the young church. One early Christian philosopher, Origen (A.D. 185–254), taught a mystical form of reincarnation as his explanation of and solution to the problem of sin. He taught also that the soul's entrance into a bodily form was a punishment; salvation occurred when the soul was forever freed from the prison of the body. Such views were similar to the ancient Hindu *moksha* and Plato's *Tenth Book of the Republic*, published four centuries before Christ. Origen, however, was eventually denounced as a heretic for his erroneous teachings (A.D. 553). But his views nonetheless had considerable influence for several centuries.[16]

What Brings Hope?

The theory of reincarnation provides hope for individuals who despair in their ambition to be good enough to merit divine approval. Even some church people find that possibility intriguing. People can work as hard as

---

[16]Hans Schwarz, *Beyond the Gates of Death: A Biblical Examination of Evidence for Life After Death* (Minneapolis: Augsburg Publishing House, 1981), p. 90. "Without any apologies Clement uses images that were usually associated with reincarnation to make plausible the belief in the resurrection. Evidently the belief in reincarnation was so familiar that its images could be used to illustrate the less familiar belief in resurrection" (p. 92).

possible in this life and then be assured that they can build on that same good foundation in a succeeding life. But no one is perfect. Everyone knows that no human being can match up to God's expectations. Is it possible to be "good enough" for God's acceptance?

To answer that dilemma, the Bible proclaims that Jesus Christ was the only One who was "good enough." He paid the price for our wrongdoing. He became our representative, our sacrifice for sin. Humanists solve the problem by denying the existence of anything outside this universe, including a perfect God. They believe in humanity, expecting human beings eventually to evolve to perfection. They maintain that there is recourse or hope completely within ourselves. In this aspect, humanism and reincarnation are similar. In reincarnation one can achieve salvation through personal evolution, as in humanism. No wonder reincarnation has become so appealing to today's self-centered, insecure masses!

Thus it is clear that *Christianity and reincarnation can not be intermixed* because they represent opposing points of view. I realized that if I was betting my life on what I believed, then I had better make sure my beliefs were correct. I knew I had to look further into these ideas.

Chapter 2

THE QUEST FOR IMMORTALITY

What is your view of death? Death is as much a part of life as is birth, but the phenomenon did not seem to preoccupy our great-grandparents as it does us. Today many people seem morbidly concerned, even fascinated, with death. In fact, when I recently counted them, I discovered more courses available on death and dying in some colleges than on human sexuality.

My Close Encounter with Death

One day, most unexpectedly, I found myself personally facing death. The experience happened after I had piloted my own plane to Indianapolis to attend a postgraduate seminar dealing with unusual heart rhythm disturbances. A fellow cardiologist flew with me. He was not a pilot, but on the trip north I showed him how to keep the faithful Aztec centered on course for the instrument flight route that we had filed earlier. At nightfall, I took over the controls. We descended in darkness, approached the runway, and landed.

The next day we awoke early to start a six o'clock jogging session around the capitol building in the downtown area. The weather was quite cold, but we were encouraged when we saw a couple of other people also out jogging in the brisk morning air.

If my body had wanted to warn me of an impending heart attack, it should have done so then. But no warning came during the half hour of exercise nor during our return flight home. My flying partner, who was to become my own doctor, later reflected, "How would I have landed the plane if you had developed that heart attack while we were flying home?" Trying to be facetious, I reminded him of several highways we had seen below us, which could have served as landing strips. He didn't think my observations funny.

A couple of days later I was awakened at 4:30 in the morning by a severe mid-chest aching, a burning pain that recurred intermittently until it forced my admission to the Diagnostic Hospital that evening. Not wanting to admit that a heart attack could happen to me, I waited until it was too late to consider bypass surgery for relief.

My physician, Dr. Charles McDonald, examined me and obtained electrocardiograms. They proved to be normal in spite of the insistent pain. Later that night a massive heart attack occurred and the expected EKG changes finally appeared. The pain became excruciating. I had never experienced anything like it before. An oxygen mask was fitted over my face, intravenous narcotics were given, and several nitroglycerin medications administered. Nothing helped. I found myself crying aloud, "God, help me! God, help me!" I thought to myself that anybody's agnosticism must soon disappear in that kind of trouble. My plaintive words then changed to "Jesus, save me! Jesus, save me!"

Strange ideas were going through my mind. I didn't care whether I lived or died—just make that terrible pain go away. I still remember my thoughts and feelings clearly. I was aware that I might be dying. I felt my heart as it started flipping intermittently into rhythms which I knew from experience with other patients were frequently a premonitory sign of impending death. On the monitor overhead I could see my own heart rhythm as it wrote a fatal type of pattern on the scope. This particular rhythm was called *ventricular tachycardia,* and it was not responding to the intravenous medications that had been given to me.

Oddly, I realized I was not afraid to die, nor was I afraid to enter another world. There was no question in my mind about the reality of life after death. I was sure of what would be coming next; I felt it in my soul. I asked myself, could this merely be the result of Christian training and beliefs? Was it the great hope mentioned in Titus 2:13? Or could this possibly be moksha, the Hindu liberation and final exaltation of the soul? I felt my soul would soon be released from my body. Or should I interpret this feeling as a death-denying reaction and nothing more? Was it, after all, only a life wish?

Several hours later, the perspiration stopped and the intense pain subsided. I realized I wasn't going to die at that time. Then I thought about all those promises I had made to God during my pain. They didn't seem important anymore. What about all those convicting thoughts about my soul? Well, they really didn't matter much, did they? Especially since I was sure I was getting well. *But wait a minute. . .* A chill came on me, a chill of realization that I had brushed closely to the realms of heaven and hell.

Direct Encounter with Death

"I don't want to die! Let go of me!"

The guard was prying the victim's fingers loose as they held fast to the bars of the cell. Another guard came to assist in wrenching the prisoner's fingers from the cold metal, while two other guards wrestled with him to control his frantic behavior. He was fighting for his life. A minister stood helplessly nearby, unsure of his duties. The prisoner, when finally pried loose, ran to the clergyman.

"Tell them not to kill me! Please tell them! Please!" the prisoner cried, his body racked by sobs and gasps. "I don't want to die!"

"Neither did that kid you killed," said the guard. "She didn't want to die either!"

And so, struggling down the hall, the group took the inmate to the electric chair. Soon the briefly dimmed lights signaled the end of his final battle for survival. There he was, slumped in the chair, the doctor listening to the chest to pronounce him dead. Where was this man's spirit—the spirit that had animated his body and was supposed to survive physical death? The age-old question haunted the witnesses. Had his spirit also died, or was it hovering in the room, living and invisible?

Our quest for immortality is reenacted daily, manifested in many different ways. It may take the form of a fierce denial of death to the end. Others, instead of fighting for life, become mesmerized by impending death:

The State of Florida trussed John Arthur Spenkelink immobile in the electric chair yesterday morning, dropped a black leather mask over his face and electrocuted him.

"He simply looked at us, he looked terrified," said Chris Rebillot, a television reporter who was one of 32 persons who watched through a window from an adjoining room. "It was just a wide, wide, wide stare."

The first surge of electricity, 2,500 volts, was administered at 10:12 a.m. Spenkelink jerked in the chair, one hand clenched into a fist. A doctor unbuttoned his white shirt, pulled up the T-shirt underneath and placed a stethoscope to his chest. The doctor stepped back and another surge of electricity was sent through the body by two anonymous executioners in black hoods.

There was another stethoscope check, another surge, the third, and at 10:18 the doctor checked for the pulse, lifted the mask, flashed his pen light in either eye and nodded to the warden that Spenkelink was dead.[1]

Pre-Death Reports

A victim of terminal illness may grasp for immortality, either by denying death directly or by undergoing a metamorphosis through various stages in the dying process.[2]

People may report unusual occurrences as death nears. Shortly before death some patients claim to see apparitions of heavenly hosts. Many of us can recall a relative who vividly described an angelic being at the foot of the bed, or a vision of friends who had previously died, beckoning for the patient to come with them. What we don't hear much about are hell-like experiences where the dying patient sees demons arrive at his bedside. The surviving family find no pleasure in relating these bad experiences described by their loved ones before death. Such stories are suppressed while the "good" ones flourish.

Certainly, not all deaths are pleasant. Deathbed witnesses, in fact, are often terrified by what they see or hear. Movie star June Havoc, for instance, told of her mother's adoration of June's sister, Louise, known to most of us as Gypsy Rose Lee. Yet, on her deathbed, the mother denounced Louise, saying, "You'll never forget

---

[1]Los Angeles *Herald Examiner*, Saturday, May 26, 1979, p. 2–A.
[2]Maurice S. Rawlings, *Before Death Comes* (Nashville: Thomas Nelson, Inc., 1980), pp. 78–80.

how I'm holding you right this minute, holding you as strongly as I can, wishing with all my heart I could take you all the way—all the way down." As she spoke, the dying mother gripped Louise in a chilling embrace. June watched speechlessly as her mother spilled out hate with her last gasps.[3]

Clinical Evidence for Reincarnation?

Have you ever seen a place or person that reminds you of something or someone you knew before—somewhere you've been in the past, for instance? I have. Does this mean that you or I lived a previous life and are recognizing a distantly familiar part of that experience? Or is it merely a coincidental look-alike?

An old farmhouse in Elmwood, Illinois, has a Gothic arched window in the front gable of the house. That house appears in the background of greeting cards, magazine covers, etc., depicting a farmer and his wife in the foreground. The original artwork, called *American Gothic*, was painted by Grant Wood. You've probably seen this picture yourself. I imagine that many people who go by that farmhouse comment that they've seen that place before. Perhaps a circumstance like this explains some experiences of déjà vu.

But how do you explain hypnotic trances in which people speak a language they do not know when awake, and describe previous-life experiences? Such a situation was recounted in *The Search for Bridey Murphy:* Bridey spoke Gaelic and recalled historical experiences in old Ireland. With such a case, you can accept a person's

---

[3]Chattanooga *News—Free Press*, Sunday, December 7, 1980, p. 1–J.

claims on faith alone—or you can examine the so-called evidence to see if it really stands the test. In my own investigations, I find that many such stories are not true. There are often alternative interpretations; even some well-known accounts have proved to be complete fabrications.

In contrast, I have interviewed people who have actually "died," experiencing clinical death but recovering through resuscitation before biological tissue death can occur.

About twenty percent of patients who have been successfully retrieved from clinical death have an experience to report after resuscitation. Of those, contrary to previously published literature, there seem to be as many bad experiences as good ones. I have chronicled interviews of this kind in my previous books. Those interviews are firsthand accounts of events occurring after death, with sequential similarity so striking that they defy fabrication—cases of accurate recall of events occurring during death, experiences in another world (not this one), and the profound impact of the event upon their own lives. Such accounts indicate that something dramatic waits beyond death's door.

In addition to those accounts, people have related experiences of near-death premonitions. Such premonitions are without any typical sequence; therefore, they are more difficult to analyze than experiences of actual clinical death. You may know someone, for example, who survived a head-on collision and whose whole life was reviewed for him or her before the impact of the accident occurred. How can a lifetime be reviewed in a split second? Is there possibly a time warp to account for this?

The Ultimate Question

Are experiences such as pre-death apparitions and life reviews conjecture or reality? What happens to you when you die? Where do you go? All through history, people have predicted life after death. Now, with modern resuscitation methods, we have produced a group of people who say they can tell us what happens when one dies. Do those reports give any valid insights into reincarnation?

No case that I know of received any verbal, visual, or other indication that the victim would return to this earth in another body. On the contrary, they had every indication that they would stay where they were assigned in the spirit world. After resuscitation they "returned" in the same body in which they left—at least they didn't look any different to me, the attending physician.

Could transition into another body be something that occurs later, when the patient enters a permanent, biological type of death? Yet the deceased's loved ones, who seemingly greeted them in the spirit world, were exactly as the dying person had last seen *them*. They were not in someone else's body.

Death occurs only once, according to the writer to the Hebrews. He said that Christ's death was sufficient to atone for all people's sins for all time and that we therefore shed our corruptible bodies only *once* (see Heb. 9:27).

It's Universal

The quest for immortality—the will to live, the desire to deny death, the drive to defeat death—is this merely a basic animal instinct for survival? Or is it an innate, indwelling foreknowledge of what is to come?

Is this age-old belief in an afterlife the cause for the emergence of most world religions, or is it the result of those religions? Why do so many patients repeatedly call out "God, help me!" during severe pain? Is such a cry for help merely the result of parental teaching, or is it an inbred recognition of the existence of a Creator?

The life wish is universal; we see its expression everywhere. Trying to outlive themselves, many people secretly wish to have a monument built to honor themselves, or a trust or memorial established in their memory. We want to live forever, any way we can.

Our modern, death-denying society has given some slippery hucksters additional products to sell. According to the *Wall Street Journal*, you can now buy a "talking tombstone." There are sixteen models to choose from. Should you care to tape a message before you die, a recording of your own voice will broadcast from the tombstone. A built-in slide projector is also an option if you wish to emphasize the memorable events of your life.

But our hopes of grandiosity dwindle when the New Testament describes the vanity of life wishes: "Yet you do not know what your life will be like tomorrow. You are just a vapor that appears for a little while and then vanishes away" (James 4:14). Pilgrims we are, but frequently without a clear purpose. To most of us, the mystery of death still represents the ultimate tragedy rather than the ultimate healing.

The proponents of medical science insist that life be prolonged at almost any cost. We physicians regard the death of our patients as a personal defeat. The oncologist who treats cancer patients often becomes intent upon continued chemotherapy in spite of inevitable death. I sometimes envision a caricature of one of these doctors opening the lid of a patient's coffin "for just one more treatment."

Like General Bullmoose from one sequence of the old "Li'l Abner" comic strips, some of us would evidently like to hibernate in the deep freeze and thus prolong our lives through reduced metabolism. As a matter of fact, there have been hopeful requests from affluent citizens that their bodies be kept frozen when they die, in anticipation that science will discover some life-preserving drug that could be administered when they're "thawed out" sometime in the future.

People still seek the proverbial fountain of youth. When he came to the shores of Florida as a Spanish explorer in the sixteenth century, Ponce de Leon was not the first to seek the secret of eternal youth. Most everyone would like to prevent the clock from moving forward. Aging is feared because it represents our gradual self-destruction. It is a process difficult to conceal; nevertheless, we try our best, spending millions of dollars each year to support a flourishing cosmetics industry. Why is it that the older we become, the younger we try to appear? As we get older we wear dashing clothes we wouldn't have thought of wearing previously. Rejuvenating our enthusiasm for sports and exercise, we may even jog a little. We turn to other procedures as well: face-lifting, breast-lifting, perhaps even derrière-lifting. We spend a lot of time looking in the mirror, hoping those aging lines will respond to Oil of Olay or cosmetic camouflage. Hair transplants, salons for fat people, health spas, beauty shops, even health foods—all are manifestations of our continuing quest for youth. Though all of this eventually fails, the quest for immortality becomes our passion. Temporary solutions become our gods as we futilely attempt to hold back the day of reckoning.

Yet all of us must face death, and in that plunge into the great mystery we "bet our life" on what we believe will happen to us when we die. On what beliefs are you betting your life? I hope that this book will help clarify the validity of your own life wish.

CHApTER 3

WORLD RELIGIONS AND THE DEVELOPMENT OF REINCARNATION

Thousands of years ago, somewhere between the Tigris and Euphrates rivers in old Persia, humankind was born. The major world religions were born in the same area, somewhere in the eastern extremity of the Fertile Crescent, the area now the crux of tension between Iraq and Iran. This cradle of civilization was known in the ancient world as Babylon.

All those religions probably began like seedlings. Some never developed into trees at all. Some died young. Some grew to huge dimensions. Some are now fully developed and reproducing; others are still sprouting. But all eventually seek answers to two questions: Is there a God? Is there life after death? Explaining the cycle of birth, death, and rebirth is a nearly universal theme of religion and mythology.

True religion began with the first humans in the Garden of Eden, but counterfeit paths to God multiplied quickly as human beings settled throughout the fertile Mesopotamian valley. The earliest religions of which we have archaeological information included the practice of some form of astrology. Most of them later developed some belief in reincarnation or transmigration.

Astrology, the oldest of the man-made religions, developed indirectly into the other religions and permeates many of them even today. The religions of traditional reincarnation include Hinduism, Buddism, Zoroastrianism, Jainism, and many subgroups that moved eastward. These religions took root in India, China, Japan, and other nations of Asia and the Far East.

The religions that developed with relation to the Bible were Judaism, Christianity, and Islam. These Semitic faiths spread westward along the Mediterranean Sea into Europe, and eventually into North and South America. In some sense both Christianity and Islam were offshoots of Judaism. All three were monotheistic: Their doctrine was based on belief in one God. Those doctrines did not include reincarnation.

Of these two groups of religions, the reincarnationists and the Semitics, let us look first at the reincarnation faiths and see how their philosophies developed.

Religions of Reincarnation

I was surprised to learn that the idea of reincarnation was so old. In some cases it grew up right along with the development of astrology. Modern researchers now suggest that some fifteen hundred years before Christ, the names of the Egyptian kings indicated belief in their ability to reincarnate. It was supposedly proof of their divinity, since reincarnation was beyond the reach of common folk. Gradually, however, the idea came to be applied to ordinary people. In the Egyptian Book of the Dead, about a dozen chapters give the appropriate spells to be recited in order to reincarnate in various forms. While Pythagoras is sometimes credited with inventing the theory of reincarnation, it is likely that he merely adapted it from these Egyptian theories of transmigration that had already been established for nearly a thousand years.

Another surprise in my journey through the religions of reincarnation was that they do not agree on how reincarnation works or even on what its goal is. As we shall see, the only common denominator in the various theories is the search for immortality: the universal life wish.

Hinduism

The Hindu religion borrowed its name from an Aryan word for the area watered by the Indus river, and for the most part, Hinduism has remained a religion of the peoples of India. Believers in that country number some 350 million, while another 20 million Hindus live in Asian and African nations and another 350,000 in the Americas.[1]

Hinduism is a vast, complex, unwieldy, and often contradictory religion. It developed over a period of several thousand years. It had no single founder but borrowed ideas, practices, and beliefs from many other religions. The Hindu religion has been called the *sanatana dharma* (eternal religion) since it claims to encompass the truth in all religions of all times. Modern Hinduism even tries to harmonize itself with Christianity, intimating that Christianity can find its full expression in Hinduism.

Five main periods of development can be seen in the history of Hinduism: Vedic (2000–600 B.C.), Reactionary (600 B.C.–A.D. 300), Puranic (A.D. 300–1200), Medieval (A.D. 1200–1750), and Modern (1750–present).

The earliest Hindu writings are called the *Vedas* (which means "knowledge" or "wisdom"). This literature contains hymns, prayers, rituals, and spells. The Vedas

---

[1]M. Thomas Starks, *Today's World Religions* (New Orleans: Insight Press, 1978), p. 33.

are variously classified as *Mantras*, or praises to the gods; *Brahmanas*, which are instructions for religious services and practices; and *Upanishads*, which philosophically and mystically discuss religious truth. The Upanishads are the springboard for later developments in Hinduism and deal primarily with *Brahman*, or what is real, and man (*atman*, or self). In the Upanishads we see a movement from simple animistic polytheism toward the later Hindu monism (belief that all reality is one essence or being).

Expansions on the Vedas include several different kinds of writings, some of which are more revered and considered closer to being divinely inspired than others.

In this second body of literature, we find the Hindu text most familiar to the West, the *Bhagavad-Gita* or "hymn to the Lord." The Bhagavad-Gita is a dialogue between a warrior-prince and his charioteer, Krishna, who is supposedly the disguised incarnation of the Hindu god, Vishnu. Their dialogue is descriptive of modern Hindu belief. It emphasizes disinterested action within one's caste as the best *yoga* (exercise) to bring one swiftly to god-consciousness. It illustrates the modern tendency to personalize Hindu deity, a move in the direction of personal monotheism (belief in one God) and henotheism (worship of one supreme God over all others).

The Hindu scriptures developed and were modified many times over thousands of years, resulting in innumerable subgroups of believers. The concepts of *karma* and *reincarnation*, however, have remained the cornerstones of all Hinduism and its splinter factions.

Karma is the cosmic law of divine retribution and is absolutely unalterable. It is the merciless cycle of cause and effect. In Hinduism, however, karma is designed ultimately to "liberate" the individual from its own clutches. This liberation is called moksha. Here's how the Hindu theory works.

Hinduism teaches that in ultimate reality "All is One." This means that everything we identify as having separate existence—whether individual personalities, cement trucks, the ocean, whatever—all are really the same thing. Everything is One, and that One is "God." The trouble begins when souls that are really part of "God" begin to identify with their individuality. Hindu doctrine teaches that the soul is not the mind, not the body, not the personality. But if it thinks it is, then everything it does will create karma. In Hinduism you are what you think, and karma is the result of thinking that you're anything else but God.

When unliberated souls are born, they are born into *maya*, the "illusion of separateness" which we Westerners call the world. All of the soul's subsequent actions produce unavoidable reactions which return to that soul in this life or the next. The karma one accumulates through taking action of any kind must eventually be burnt off. The events of one's life reflect that process, meted out as one's station and fate in this life.

Karma does not stop, however, with only one life. The soul is born again and again (reincarnated or transmigrated) into the position in life that one's previous karmic debt dictates. Only when that karmic debt has been fully paid through countless lifetimes can the soul cease its cycle of birth and death and come to rest in the "oneness" of the supreme god, Brahman, the *nirvana* of nothingness.

It has probably occurred to you that in this system, while a person is burning off old karma, he or she is all the while creating new karma which will have to be burnt off in another life. That is true. That's why the holiest person in Hinduism is the *sanyasi*, or renunciate.

The renunciate has left the world of maya and spends all his time in meditation, attempting to merge his consciousness with Brahman. In that way he creates no karma. Also, it is believed that intense meditation can burn up many lifetimes of karma in a very short time.

But for the "rank and file" Hindu, concerned about family and survival, karmic law marches on. He can only hope—or pray to the gods—that in his next life he will be able to give more time to spiritual practice. Unless he is willing to give up all emotional attachment to friends and loved ones, and all desire for personal survival, his fate in this life is sealed.

Although modern Indian law has forbidden discrimination by the caste system, the law has been unable to deal with karmic logic, which states that one's birth into a particular caste reflects one's karmic debt: something that person deserves.

Hinduism Today

One evening during hospital rounds I sat at the bedside of a patient from India. The owner of several textile manufacturing concerns near Calcutta, he was visiting his son, an engineer at DuPont's large plant in our city. He had agreed to enlighten me about the religious life of Hinduism today as he knew it. He was a very patient and diligent teacher. He began speaking slowly in a very cultured voice.

"Because our god can never be realized by anyone not pure in heart, I start each day with a ritual prayer hymn we call a *puja*. In my country I have a *guru* or teacher who helps to guide me into the divine life through meditations we do in the *ashrams* of our city. If I can stay true to my karma, I will do better in my next life as a result of my actions in this life.

"Bound up with the concept of karma, however, is *samsara*, the concept of birth and rebirth on a 'wheel of life.' The soul is considered eternal and existing in each of us from the beginning of time, appearing through the different lives we lead."

"What do you mean by 'wheel of life'?" I interrupted.

"This wheel of life is the game of life, the process of birth, death, and rebirth which you call reincarnation. It can be terminated only by liberation or release, the process we call moksha. This chain of birth and rebirth can then be broken, and the bondage of the soul to these different bodies can be finally stopped. The good Hindu longs for release from this life because it is at that time that he realizes oneness with god. This is called nirvana."

I shifted my position a bit and asked, "What about judgment in the next life?"

"All religions are concerned with eternity and with existence beyond physical death," he replied. "But Hinduism is concerned with the eternal existence of the soul rather than with the soul's relationship with god; *god* is more of a Christian concept. While the soul is imprisoned in the body during life, it is subject to impurity. But since the soul itself is not responsible for this imprisonment, it is not subject to sin. Therefore, if the soul is not subject to sin, it is not subject to judgment; and if it is not subject to judgment, then it does not require the salvation that your Christian religion would suggest."

"Let's talk about déjà vu," I said. "Does that fit into the picture?"

He paused. "It is true that many people will uncannily recall something they have seen in a previous life. Those experiences help to prove that previous lives have existed for that person. In that sense, these reminders can be a form of judgment. That is to say, we believe the same thing you Christians believe: 'What you sow is what you reap.' "

He seemed to have ready answers, so I posed another question. "How does reincarnation work? What actually happens when you die?"

After considering his response for a while, he answered, "When a man dies, his soul comes out of his body and immediately enters the body of a newborn babe. If the man has led a good life, he is born again into a higher caste. If he has led a bad life, he is born into a lower caste. That is the result of his karma. He could also be born sick and suffer all of his life as punishment for his previous deeds. Some of our people believe that deeds could be bad enough to cause rebirth as an animal—a dog, for instance, or a worm or a fly."

"I assume you would try to avoid that by doing good works to earn a better place in the next life?"

"Yes, but only in part. It's more important to develop a type of god-consciousness through meditation, which is a form of yoga. What we call yoga is an exercise, either spiritual or physical, that is designed to bring one into god-consciousness. I use a meditative yoga, a means of worship in which the mind is emptied so that everything can be devoted to concentration on god and on our oneness with him."

"Do you mean that you and god are one and the same?" I asked.

"Yes, you could say that—just as you and I are really one. We call this the *truth of identification*. For instance, I am you and you are me. As the god Krishna said to a student, as recorded in the Bhagavad-Gita, 'Never have I not been, never hast thou not been, and never shall the time come when we shall not be.' The atman, or soul, is the only true self. All else is illusion.

The second truth is karma, which we discussed."

The more answers he supplied, the more interested I became.

"Is that why the rich do not help the poor very much in your country? Because that person may be suffering punishment for his bad karma or fate of a previous life?"[2]

He did not answer that question. "A third truth," he went on, "is reincarnation. Each of us will live again on this earth and work out his destiny, reaping the reward of his previous acts until he can eventually merge into the soul of god."

"By that you mean that it is up to the individual to save himself?"

"That is correct. Through meditation we find god in ourselves. God and ourselves have been one all along. It is up to us to 'save' ourselves, if you want to call it that, not only through good works, but by finding god within us."

I reviewed in my mind what I thought he had said. I am god! And god is me! Since there is no sin, there is no hell, and since there is no hell, no salvation is required. How opposed this was to Christianity.

Although I didn't agree with the views of this learned man, I was honored that he would share them with me. I could understand why my patient was proud to be a Hindu. I had read some of the beautiful poetry in the Upanishads. There I found the Hindu's path:

> *He who sees himself in all beings*
> *And all beings in himself,*
> *He enters the supreme Brahma—*
> *By this means and no other.*

---

[2]Some rich Indians (notably the Jains) do help the poor, as part of their yoga of disinterested action on behalf of others. Such action is seen as a path to god.

To me that seems the crux of the matter. My Hindu patient told me that since human beings are basically good, they will eventually save themselves. Christianity asserts that since human beings are basically evil, they need salvation from a source external to themselves.

But salvation unto what? The Hindu "salvation" promises an oblivion of nothingness when nirvana is reached. The Christian salvation promises eternal, personal fellowship with God for the individual believer.

Buddhism

Buddhism, a giant offspring of Hinduism, left India to dominate the Far East. In recounting the relentless march of world religions, it helps to remember that Buddhism came into existence almost six hundred years *before* Christ, while Islam arose about six hundred years *after* Christ. Although these three religions share worldwide appeal, Buddhism was, by several centuries, the first of the religions to become international.

Buddhism is the predominant religion of the Far East, that vast expanse of land that stretches from Manchuria to Java and from Central Asia to the islands of Japan.[3] The sacred book of Buddhists is called the *Tripitaka*, which means the "three baskets of wisdom."

Buddha was a man whose story is interesting indeed. He was born about 563 B.C. on the border of Nepal, 130 miles north of the city of Benares. Although the name *Buddha* means "the enlightened one," his real name was Siddhartha Gautama.

---

[3]Joseph Gaer, *How the Great Religions Began* (New York: New American Library, 1956), p. 22.

It is claimed that Siddhartha represents the last in a series of over five hundred and fifty reincarnations or different lifetimes of one soul. During those lifetimes he suffered greatly, fulfilled every perfection, and won his goal of ultimate "enlightenment"—both for himself and for all humankind. He not only magnanimously abandoned his heritage and wealth in an aristocratic family, but he also abandoned his wife and son to seek the secret reasons for life. He started his quest by becoming a hermit.

He stated that he received his enlightenment while sitting under a fig tree. That enlightenment included the First Law of Life: from Good must come Good, and from Evil must come Evil. After spending many days under the tree, Siddhartha went to Benares and found five fellow monks with whom to share his enlightenment. He said, "If these gods have no power to change anything in the world, then we should not be praying to them, nor should they be worshiped. If man does good, the results will be good, and if he does evil, the results will be evil, and all the gods in India cannot change that."

"That sounds true," the monks agreed.

"Now, if that is really true," said the Buddha, "it must follow, as day follows night, that the Vedas, which tell people how to pray and how to sacrifice, are not holy. Our priests say to you that the Vedas and every word in them are holy, but I say to you that the Vedas are not Sacred Books at all."

"Who do you think created the world?" the monks then inquired.

"The world was not created by anyone. The world was always in existence. The world will always be in existence. It never will come to an end, because it stands to reason that anything that has no end also has no beginning."

Further divorcing his new followers from Hinduism, the Buddha continued: "There are two extremes, my friends, to keep away from. One is the life of pleasure, which is selfish and ignoble. The other is the life of self-torture. That, too, is unworthy. These two extremes do not lead to the Good Life."

"Then what is the road that one should follow?" the monks asked.

"Follow the middle path," the Buddha replied.

"How can one find the middle path?"

"By following the eightfold path."

"What is the eightfold path?"

"The eightfold path teaches the eight rules of life: right belief, right resolve, right speech, right behavior, right occupation, right effort, right contemplation, right concentration."

The Buddha concluded by giving the monks the five commandments of uprightness that he had received:

Do not kill.
Do not steal.
Do not lie.
Do not commit adultery.
Do not become intoxicated at any time.

Thereafter, the monks concluded: "This is surely wisdom, and Siddhartha Gautama has certainly become the enlightened one, the 'Buddha,' for he has set in motion the wheel of the true law of life. The law that teaches all mankind that the world is ruled by justice."[4]

At the age of eighty, the Buddha became suddenly very ill. On his deathbed he told his followers, "You have my word, my explanations of truth, and the laws I have

---

[4]Ibid., pp. 37,38.

given you. Let them be your guide. Buddha has not left you." After saying these words, he died. The year was 483 B.C., over 2400 years ago.

Although the Buddha himself preached against images, his followers continued to set up images in many temples, making Buddha himself an idol. Buddhism grew into a significant world religion, based on reincarnation and the eight-fold path. Today, Buddhism continues to be a major influence in world religions, teaching its followers how people ought to live in order to obtain the Good Life. The Good Life results in an improvement in the next reincarnated life.

The reincarnation teaching of Buddhism is similar to that of Hinduism, but there are some key differences. The *Dhammapada* (*dhamma* means "discipline"; *pada* is "path"), the most popular and influential of the Buddhist literature, sums it up like this:

All that we are is the result of what we have thought; all that we are is founded on our thoughts and formed of our thoughts . . .
Who shall overcome this earth? And who the sphere of Yama, the god of death? And who the world of the happy gods? And who shall choose the steps on the Path of Law even as the gardener culls the choicest blooms? The disciple will overcome this earth. Also Yama loka (the realm of death). Also the sphere of the gods. The disciple chooses to take steps on the Path of Law . . .

In Buddhism, as in Hinduism, you are what you think. But instead of offering a meditation in which you think of yourself as God, Buddhism emphasizes *dharma*—the intrinsic law of your being. Discovery of his dharma keeps a disciple on the middle path. Thus karma is not so much burned off as it is fulfilled. Only then is a person liberated. If one creates enough good karma, he will be reincarnated as a god in some blissful realm; if too much bad karma, as a demon in a hellish world. The demonic person will then have to wait for the opportunity to reincarnate as a human being in order to become liberated.

In Tibetan Buddhism, the *Bodhisattva* is the soul who already has attained liberation himself, but who has vowed not to enter nirvana until all beings have been freed from the wheel of deaths and births. The Bodhisattva voluntarily reincarnates. The Dalai Lama of Tibetan Buddhism is supposedly such a soul.

Jainism

Jainism is another cult or division of reformed Hinduism, and it also incorporates belief in reincarnation. Jainism developed over a period of two or three hundred years, beginning twenty-five hundred to three thousand years ago. Various individuals helped in its development, among them Siddhartha (a contemporary of Siddhartha Gautama), Bahubalia, and Mahavira (a Hindu name meaning "great hero"). Tradition credits Mahavira with the formal establishment of the Jainist sect, which today claims three million followers, almost all of whom are wealthy Indians. Jainism is now divided into three sects: The Digambara, the Shvetambara, and the Sthanakavasi. The various sacred scriptures of these three sects are collectively called *Agamas* (precepts).

The goal of a Jain (a word meaning "conqueror") is to achieve moksha, reaching a state of nirvana through extreme self-discipline and ascetism. The Jains do not believe in a supreme creator or God, believing instead that the universe itself is eternal and that the law of karma is the supreme law of all existence. The soul of a thing is its life, which is bound by material existence. The goal of the soul is to satisfy its karmic debt and be forever free from nonlife (the material world). Since there is no divine being in Jainism, this liberation can be accomplished only by the individual working within the law of karma through successive births until he finally satisfies his debt and reaches nirvana.

The Jain practice for which its followers are best known is the law of *ahimsa*, or noninjury. This rule is obeyed so strictly that Jain monks sweep the road in front of them so that they won't kill any insects. Jain mothers very carefully pick the lice out of their children's hair, making sure not to harm the lice. Jains are strict vegetarians. Because they believe that plants, too, have souls, Jains confess and do penance for their sin of eating them everyday. The wealth of most Jains is a result of their being restricted to occupations least likely to involve taking life: banking, investments, and so on.

A survey of the legendary life of Mahavira illustrates the Jain path to salvation. Born of royal parents in 600 B.C. in Vesali, Mahavira was twenty-eight years old when he saw the slow death of his mother and father from self-imposed starvation. This was considered a holy death when purposely done. Loss of his parents so grieved the prince that he took the vows of a beggar monk and also a vow of silence: "I shall not utter a single word from this moment forward, for twelve years hence."

It is said that one day a shepherd offered Mahavira food in exchange for watching his flock. When the shepherd returned, Mahavira couldn't explain that a missing lamb had been killed by a wolf. He could offer no explanation because of his vow of silence. The shepherd then started beating Mahavira until blood began to flow. Suddenly realizing that Mahavira was a large man, the shepherd stopped beating him and looked at him with growing fear.

"You are the first man I've met who would not protect himself. Why didn't you run away? You must indeed be a very holy man!"

Mahavira didn't answer, but got up and walked away.

"This monk has taught me a great lesson," the shepherd said. "Silence is stronger than words!"

Mahavira, wandering off in the other direction, thought, "This incident has taught me a great lesson. Humility is better than Pride; and Peace stronger than Anger."[5]

During those twelve years of silence, Mahavira did much thinking. After that period was completed, he started preaching. "How are we to do away with all the suffering we see? By giving up all desire? No! When a man gives up desires, then he can't prepare himself for the greatest happiness of the soul, nirvana itself."

"What, then, is the way to nirvana?" the people asked.

"The way to nirvana," Mahavira answered, "is through the three jewels of the soul, which are right conviction, right knowledge, and right conduct."

"Since you do not believe that sacrifices to the gods or saying prayers will do any good, how may we find nirvana?" they continued.

He answered, "Not in prayer, not in sacrifice, nor in idol worship will you find forgiveness and the way to the Good Life. Only by doing good can you reach nirvana. Within yourselves lies salvation."[6]

Mahavira, like Buddha, believed that all living things contain souls and that if a man lived a bad life, he would be reborn either as some lowly animal, or worse, as an insignificant vegetable or plant. He also believed that there were "seven hells," built in layers, one below the

---

[5]Ibid., p. 50.
[6]Ibid.

other and located somewhere below the surface of the earth. The worst hell was at the lowest level.

At the time when there were about fourteen thousand monks in his brotherhood, Lord Mahavira died. Although the religion grew in size, it has been confined largely to India.

Zoroastrianism

From Babylonia (modern Iraq and Iran), the land of the stargazers, came still another religion, Zoroastrianism, begun by the prophet Zoroaster (Zarathustra) in the sixth century B.C. Zoroaster accomplished much in his lifetime, destroying the magic and idol worship then prominent in Babylonia. The book of his teachings was called the *Avesta*, and the priests were called *magi*, using magic in their communion with their god. (That is the source of the same word we use today.) Zoroastrianists, also called Parsees, believe in both a heaven and hell, the existence of life after death. They worship one god called Ahura-Mazda.

Zoroaster taught that human souls are eternal and infinite. These spirits of the higher sphere descend to birth as humans. If a person is distinguished in knowledge and sanctity on earth, he returns above and becomes an empyreal sovereign. Attaining perfection, a person beholds the beatific vision of the Light of lights. If people lead a life of vice and depravity, however, they are separated from the primitive source of life and become evil spirits. The imperfectly good migrate from one body to another until, by enough good words and deeds, they are set free from matter and become higher ranking spirits.

It is interesting that Zoroastrianism was the official religion of the Babylonians during the time the Jews were held captive in Babylonia (586–445 B.C.). Those two religions thus coexisted for many years. Almost all Zoroastrianists left the country later, however, under religious persecution. Most of them retreated to India about thirteen hundred years ago when the Arabs conquered what was then Persia, forcing the remaining members into their own religion of Islam at the threat of death. As a result, only about one hundred thousand Zoroastrianists remain in the world today, most of them in India.

Confucianism, Taoism, and Shintoism

At the same time that the Buddha and Lord Mahavira were establishing their great splinter groups from Hinduism, three other philosophical beliefs were emerging in China and Japan. They were Confucianism, Taoism, and Shintoism. Although they should be considered more philosophies than religions, they will be briefly mentioned here because of their frequent incorporation of Buddhist thought and belief in reincarnation.

Confucius (Kung Fu-Tzu) was born in the Chinese province known today as Shantung. His famous *Four Books* preserve his system of ethics, philosophical speculations, rituals, and an accumulation of ancient wisdom he felt important. His writings speak little of a supreme deity or deities and confine themselves to promoting moral conduct and harmony among human beings. He popularized the Chinese form of the Golden Rule, that one should do only what one would like others to do to oneself. A later development from Confucius' original teachings is the elaborate ancestor worship of many oriental religious movements. Confucius himself, however, avoided discussion of metaphysical subjects.

Taoism (pronounced *Dowism*) arose contemporarily with Confucius, but there is little historic validity to the claim that it was started by a man named Lao-Tzu. Its true origin remains shrouded in myth. Lao-Tzu is the supposed author of the Taoist work *Tao-te King*, or *The Way and Moral Principle*. The cornerstone of Taoism is the belief that all existence is in a state of constant flux, and therefore one cannot come to an accurate knowledge or comprehension of reality through conventional means. One simply knows or doesn't know. *Tao* is the way, the path, or the eternal principle by which all of creation is ordered. The way of the universe, according to Taoism, is to live with contentment, patience, reticence, and flexibility. One aphorism of the *Tao-te King* is this: "Highest good is like water, in that it always excels in taking the lowest place."

Proverbially, Lao-Tzu himself tells us that we can never learn anything about this Tao "if we do not already know all about it."

"They who know do not tell, and they who tell do not know," he wrote in the *Tao-te King*.

The Taoist attitude toward the wheel of births and deaths is that in the beginning we were blended in the one great, featureless mass. The mass evolved spirit, spirit evolved form, and form evolved life. Life, in turn, evolved death. Thus the end becomes the beginning. Humankind, like nature, has seasons that cycle endlessly. To blend with the cycle without effort is to become one with the Tao and so find fulfillment.

The Chinese have long been known as ancestor worshipers. To them the dead are considered as real as the living; to know what has happened to one's forebears after death is important. Neither Taoism nor Confucianism answered such questions. The Chinese eventually became fascinated with the teachings of Buddha from neighboring countries. Buddhism slowly became known all over China, mingling with Confucianism and other religions.

In Japan, meanwhile, Shintoism (which means "The Way of the Good Spirit") was becoming established. It has since grown to about thirty million adherents. Although the founder is unknown, the "records of the ancients" are contained in several religious works, one of which is called the *Kojiki*.

Besides worshiping nature gods and spirits, the Japanese also worshiped their *Mikado*, or ruler, as a god. He was considered the grandson of the sun goddess, so that the forty-two hundred islands comprising Japan today became known as the "Land of the Rising Sun." Buddhist ideas about reincarnation found their way into Shintoism.

The Semitic Faiths

Belief in reincarnation is one of the common denominators in most Eastern religious sects. The religious expressions we have briefly discussed here, from Hinduism through Shintoism, have all incorporated some belief in reincarnation or transmigration.

While those faiths were developing, Judaism, Islam, and Christianity were being established. Their original tenets were in direct opposition to the ideas of karma, reincarnation, and a nonpersonal God. The similarities of—and differences between—the Semitic faiths are striking. Let us take a short digression to complete our discussion of early world religions.

Judaism

Judaism, the oldest of the great monotheistic religions, had its beginnings long ago in the land of the Chaldees. There, in the city of Ur, at the tip of the Fertile Crescent and not far from the birthplace of Zoroaster, lived a man named Terah some four thousand years ago. He was a direct descendant of Noah—a worshiper of Jehovah—through Shem, but the city of Ur was the capital of a land of idol worshipers. At the behest of his son Abram, Terah left the land of the Chaldees with his family for the land of Canaan. Terah died in the city of Haran, at which point Jehovah promised to make Abram a great nation. Abram took his wife, Sarai, and his brother's son, Lot, into the land promised him by Jehovah.[7]

After eleven years of waiting for Jehovah to give him a son, at the suggestion of the aging and barren Sarai, Abram had a son through his wife's handmaid, Hagar. Abram was eighty-six years old. The son's name was Ishmael.

But Jehovah appeared to Abram again when Abram was ninety-nine and changed his name to Abraham ("the father of many nations"). Sarai (now called Sarah) conceived and bore a son whom they named Isaac, the first legitimate son of Abraham. In this way, through Ishmael, the Arabic race was born (see the following section on *Islam*). Through Isaac, the Jewish race was born. Isaac had a son called Jacob, renamed Israel by God, and since that time all of the children of Jacob have been known as the children of Israel and have been called

---

[7]For a more detailed account of Judaism's origins, read Genesis 11:10–21:21.

Israelites. From Jacob came twelve sons who fathered the twelve tribes of Israel.

The mothers of the two half-brothers Ishmael and Isaac never got along and their offspring, the Arabs and the Jews, although half-cousins, have hated each other down through all of history.

Judaism was established through Abraham when he received God's covenant for his descendants, although many Jews believe that their foundation stone was not laid until Moses first received the Ten Commandments directly from Jehovah on Mount Sinai. This occurred somewhere near the thirteenth century B.C.

After a time of bondage in Egypt, the Israelites returned to the land promised by Jehovah—Canaan—and built the Holy City of Jerusalem. There they were ruled by judges, who were also their military leaders. After three hundred years of this type of rule, the twelve tribes of Israel asked for a king, and reluctantly God designated a rural boy named Saul. He was followed by kings David and Solomon.

After Solomon died, the kingdom was divided: Israel, composed of ten tribes, to the north, and Judah, with two tribes, to the south. Because of their unfaithfulness to Jehovah, both kingdoms were conquered by foreign invaders.

Two hundred years after the death of Solomon, the Assyrians conquered Israel, and its people were taken captive to other lands. Many legends have since been told about these people, but they disappeared completely from history. There has never been a trace of them anywhere, and they are now referred to as the "Ten Lost Tribes of Israel."

Judah fell to the Babylonians in 597 B.C., and the leadership was taken into captivity. The temple was burned and the people carried away in 587–586 B.C.

The Jews never fully regained autonomy until May 14, 1948, when Israel was declared an independent state. Jerusalem was restored to their complete control on June 10, 1967. Traditionally, the Jews have looked for the appearance of a conquering Messiah who will again establish the Jews as a ruling nation, and Hassidic Jews still can be seen praying daily at the Wailing Wall in Jerusalem for this conquering Messiah to appear.

As opposed to Hinduism, which developed over a span of four hundred years, Judaism was established by the one God, Jehovah, who initiated relationships with His people, beginning with Abraham. In His dealings with His people—through His appearances, His law, and His prophets—Jehovah always spoke about one life, one death, and a definite afterlife.

By the time of Christ, however, some Jews had incorporated various theories of reincarnation into their beliefs. As the Jewish historian Josephus described the situation in the first century A.D., there were primarily three camps concerning the question of afterlife: the Sadducees, who rejected any notion of the immortality of the soul; the Essenes, who believed in bodily resurrection (Josephus tended erroneously to equate their beliefs to the Greek notion of a spiritual immortality of the soul akin to reincarnation), and the Pharisees, who are quoted as saying every soul is "imperishable, but the soul of good alone passes into another body. . . ."[8]

What is one of the most apparent references to belief in reincarnation among the Jews occurs in Matthew 16:14 after Jesus asks His disciples who men say He is. "And they said, Some say John the Baptist; and others, Elijah; but still others, Jeremiah, or one of the

---

[8]Hans Schwartz, *Beyond the Gates of Death* (Minneapolis: Augsburg, 1981), p. 86.

prophets." Similar references are found in Matthew 17:10–13 and 27:47. However, there was evidently a widespread belief among the Jews (see 2 Esdras 6:26, for example) that certain Old Testament people had not died but had been taken directly up to heaven and would return at the end time when their conquering Messiah appears.

Reincarnational teaching has continued to be found among some Jewish teachers and philosophers. The Cabula, a Jewish mystical philosophical system, for instance, includes a belief in reincarnation.

Although belief in reincarnation can be found among some groups of Jews, it is conspicuously absent from their scriptures themselves. Hans Schwartz explains, "it is remarkable that within a world abounding with ideas about immortality and reincarnation, the Old Testament does not advocate these commonly-held beliefs.[9]

Islam

The story of the development of the Islamic faith is intriguing. For centuries, Muslims have claimed that Ishmael, the son of Abraham by the handmaid, Hagar, was the firstborn and that therefore the Arabs inherited the covenant of God to be the Chosen People. (The Jews, on the other hand, say that God made His covenant through Isaac, Abraham's legitimate son.)

According to the ancient Muslim story, Hagar seated herself on a rock in the desert after fleeing from Abraham's household and Sarah's wrath. She started weeping for fear that she and her child would die of thirst in the desert. While the mother was weeping, little Ishmael is said to have kicked the sand in disgust and, at that exact

---

[9]*Ibid.*, p. 88.

spot where he kicked the earth, fresh water suddenly sprung forth. This came to be known as the Spring of Ishmael, also called the *Zemzem*. Near here, Abraham supposedly came and built a temple in honor of the occasion. The temple, called the *Kaaba*, is one of the most holy places in the Sacred City of Mecca, also called the City of God. It is in the direction of this city that Muslims must face in their prayers from all over the world, and it is to this city that they must come in their annual pilgrimages to drink the sacred waters from Ishmael's well.

In A.D. 570 Muhammad was born to one of the aristocratic families in Mecca. As he grew older, his occupation of sheepherder changed to that of camel driver. As a caravan leader, he found himself favored among the merchants of Mecca and married a wealthy widow, Kadijah by name. She was forty years of age and had three children by a former marriage; he was twenty-five. Muhammad subsequently became one of the richest merchants in Mecca.

His wife's cousin, Waraka, had accepted the Jewish faith and often read the Bible to Muhammad. Already familiar with the teachings of Jesus in the New Testament from his many caravan travels, Muhammad was reflecting one day upon the needs of his people when an angel, identifying himself as Gabriel, handed Muhammad a golden tablet.

The angel commanded, "Read the tablet."

"But I cannot read!" exclaimed Muhammad.

"Yes, you can read," the angel retorted.

It is said that Muhammad, who had never learned to read, immediately began reading aloud from the golden tablet with ease.

Later, Muhammad returned home and told Kadijah about this new revelation from heaven. She, in turn, encouraged him to await further appearances of this angel Gabriel. They did occur, and each time Gabriel appeared, there were new messages from heaven which Muhammad recorded on paper. These subsequently became the chapters of the Sacred Book of the Koran.

Muhammad began preaching "La ilaha illa Allah Muhammad rasul Allah," which meant, "There is no god but Allah and Muhammad is the prophet of Allah!" His followers he called Muslims or "True Believers." His other teachings were simple: "Give up idolatry, do not steal, do not lie, do not slander, and never become intoxicated." He then chose twelve apostles to spread Islam through preaching.

As he grew older, Muhammad continued to dream of a world empire ruled by Islam and fostered by the sword. He stated, "I, the last of the prophets, am sent with the sword! The sword is the key to heaven and hell! All who draw it in the cause of the Faith will be rewarded!" Although the sword was drawn in many countries to spread the cause of Islam, it was not drawn against the Jews when Islam overran Palestine. Instead, those who were not Muslims were forced to pay taxes, thus bearing the burden of government expense.

Upon Muhammad's death in A.D. 632 (he is said to have ascended into heaven on the same rock where Abraham almost sacrificed his son Isaac), the leadership was assumed by Abu Bekar, who further spread the Islamic gospel through the Holy Wars. He was the first to be called the *Caliph*, which means "The Shadow of God on Earth." The capital of Islam was moved to Damascus, then to Syria, and subsequently to the Persian capital of Bagdad.

Since that time, the number of Muslims in the world has increased to over one-seventh of the entire population, and next to Christianity, it is one of the most active, fastest-growing, and powerful religions in existence, traveling from the Mediterranean countries to the Persian Gulf, to India and China, finally to Europe, Spain, and now America. As it began to spread beyond Arabia, it brought under its rule different peoples like the Negroes, Kurds, Caucasians, Monguls, Chinese, and Hindus, so that today there are over one hundred and fifty sects of Islam, including the offshoot known as the Black Muslims.

Muslims believe in one God—Allah. Instead of reincarnation, they believe in one life on earth and one judgment, a spirit world of heaven for true believers, and Seven Terrible Hells for the nonbelievers. They believe in the prophets of Adam, Noah, Abraham, Moses, and Jesus, but the greatest of all is Muhammad.

Christianity

Like Judaism and Islam, Christianity is based on the ideas of a personal God and accountability (in the form of punishment or salvation) for one life lived here on earth. It is the only religion whose founder claims to be prophet, priest, and king. Jesus of Nazareth was a Jew, a descendant of Abraham, Isaac, and Jacob, and claimed to be the only begotten Son of God—man and God at the same time. He lived a sinless life for thirty years on earth, fulfilling the Law and prophecies of the Jewish Scriptures. He was then crucified by the religious leaders of His day—though He had done no wrong. He arose from the dead and will return to the earth one day to rule over all peoples.

Christianity is the only religion established by a leader who claimed deity. It is the only religion founded on an empty tomb. The founders of all other religions are known as being *dead*, and pilgrimages to their graves can be made to pay homage to their memory. Christianity is based on the concept of God revealing Himself in the form of man, who had the power of doing miracles and controlling the natural forces of the earth. It is based on a claim of resurrection from the dead and is revealed through the Bible, which has a distinctive insignia not found in the books of all other religions—namely, fulfilled prophecy.

Just as the full importance of the Old Testament's not advocating reincarnation can best be seen when set against its cultural background, so the New Testament's stress on the resurrection of the body is most significant when set against the popular Greek beliefs of the day. A number of Greek philosophers taught reincarnation, but it gained widest acceptance due to the teachings of Plato. Pythagoras and Meandes also propagated it.

Jesus Christ, however, taught a one-time resurrection of the body and soul. He specifically acknowledged that He was the Son of God, not the reincarnation of any earlier prophet, and laid to rest charges that He was Elijah by appearing *with* Elijah (see Matt. 17:1–5,12). And although there were differences between His body before and after His resurrection, Christ's resurrection body was clearly His own, for He showed Thomas the nail prints in His hands and the wound in His side (see John 20:24–27).

The risen Christ is said to be the "first fruits of those who are asleep" (1 Cor. 15:20,23) and Paul makes it very clear (see 1 Cor. 15:35–49) that Christians will be raised in a new body. This new body, however, will be the believer's own body and he will be recognizable. The New Testament stands out from its cultural background by its emphasis on the importance of the body and its teaching that the body—not just the soul—will be resurrected and live forever.

In the early days of the Christian faith, however, there were those who were influenced by Greek philosophy and tried to reinterpret Christ's teachings on the resurrection. The apostle Paul's letter to the Colossians is a vigorous attack on the Gnostics, who were advocating that for some believers on earth the resurrection had already occurred.

Summary

In our short overview of world religions, we have seen a basic conflict developing. Out of astrology grew a conglomerate of religions based in some fashion on the concepts of karma, reincarnation, and a more abstract concept of "god" and man. The Semitic faiths were established on the premise of one supreme, all-knowing God who communicated and dealt in a personal way with His children, and who created each member of humanity with one specific time of birth and death and a definite afterlife in either heaven or hell. Despite the tenants of the pure teachings of the Semitic religions, believers on the fringes of these faiths—frequently those influenced by other philosophies and beliefs—have sometimes tried to incorporate theories of reincarnation into their beliefs.

Modern teaching about reincarnation comes to us not from Greek philosophers but from Oriental religions. As recently as 1911, when there was little Oriental influence on Western thinking, the Encyclopaedia Britannica was able to report under the entry, *Metempsychosis*, "outside the somewhat narrow circle of Theosophists there is little disposition to accept the doctrine"[10] of reincarna-

---

[10]The Encyclopaedia Britannica, Vol. XVIII (New York: The Encyclopaedia Britannica Company, 1911), p. 260.

tion. Today, however, its influence is much more pervasive.

Christianity, although a worldwide religion, has found most of its adherents in the Western world. What appeal, if any, do exotic Eastern religious teachings have to the Western mind? When did reincarnation teaching come to America, and what are the forms it has taken since it arrived? As we shall see, the theory of reincarnation has been propagated in this country for a long time. Today it is spreading more rapidly than ever, being taught not only by the imported Eastern religions but by a vast array of home-grown new religions as well.

Chapter 4

REINCARNATION COMES TO AMERICA

It is impossible to pinpoint exactly how or when reincarnation teaching came to America. There has never been a "society of reincarnationists." Instead, the theory of rebirth has often accompanied a variety of popular movements that have developed throughout this country's history. What is certain, however, is that some form of the teaching has been here since the advent of European settlers.

The European renaissance of the fifteenth and sixteenth centuries was marked by a revival of Platonism and Plotinism (Neoplatonism). With that revival, reincarnation came into vogue in European philosophy. Also during the sixteenth century, the first major wave of colonization of the New World took place. It is probable that some of the early colonists held ideas about life after death that were influenced by the new popularity of reincarnation. We can see examples of a developed idea of reincarnation very early in America's history.

Benjamin Franklin (1706–90) wrote, "When I see nothing annihilated and not a drop of water wasted, I cannot suspect the annihilation of souls, or believe that [God] will suffer the daily waste of millions of minds ready made that now exist, and put himself to the continual trouble of making new ones."

In 1824, Unitarians in America became enthralled with a celebrated Hindu leader, Ram Mohun Roy. Roy had supposedly adopted Unitarianism while holding to his own religion and Buddhism as well.

In 1836, a group of young Unitarians openly revolted against "the corpse-cold Unitarianism" of their Harvard associates. Part of their disagreement was over the continuity of the soul's life after death. Led by Ralph Waldo Emerson, Frederic Hedge, and George Ripley, they founded the Transcendental Club of America which propagated the belief in the continuity of life. They studied the Platonic philosophers in the original Greek and obtained rare copies of the first English translations of the Bhagavad-Gita, Upanishads, Vedas, and other sacred writings of Eastern religion. Other Transcendentalists included Henry David Thoreau, James Freeman Clarke, and Henry Wadsworth Longfellow.

The Theosophical Society

Perhaps the most influential movement based on Eastern religion was the Theosophical Society. Founded in New York City in 1875, the movement soon had centers in the major cities of Europe, North America, and India. The Theosophical Society began under the leadership of Helena Petrovna Blavatsky, a Russian noblewoman who had studied in India and Tibet. Other chief founders were Henry S. Olcott and William Q. Judge. On May 10, 1890, two days after Blavatsky's death, the New York *Herald* said this in an editorial:

No one in the present generation, it may be said, has done more toward reopening the long sealed treasures of Eastern thought, wisdom, and philosophy. No one has done so much toward elucidating that profound wisdom-religion . . . whose scope and depth have so astonished the Western world. . . . Madame Blavatsky has made her mark upon the time.

Some other popular proponents of a Westernized form of reincarnation include the Unity School of Christianity, the Church of Religious Science, almost all of the other mind-science religions, and most of the spiritist cults. In fact, spiritist churches now seem to outnumber orthodox churches in some larger cities. The Los Angeles telephone directory, for example, makes it appear that way.

The Theosophical Society, though born in Ameria, actually served to revive interest in reincarnation in the Orient. Many Hindus had begun to lose faith in their religion as a result of the influence of missionaries and materialistic science. They were reacquainted with reincarnation teaching through the zeal of the Theosophists.

A notable example of this was Mahatma Gandhi, who did not even read the Bhagavad-Gita until he lived in England as a young man. There he came across two Theosophists who not only encouraged him to read the Gita but also introduced him to Madame Blavatsky. He subsequently read Blavatsky's *Key to Theosophy*, which stimulated his interest in the other sacred books of Hinduism. "This," he wrote, "disabused me of the notion fostered by the missionaries that Hinduism was rife with superstition."

Ramakrishna

Just two years after Madame Blavatsky's death, Swami Vivekananda arrived in the United States in 1893 as a delegate to the Parliament of Religions in Chicago. Born in Calcutta in 1863, Vivekananda was a devotee of

Sri Ramakrishna, one of the greatest prophets of modern Hinduism.

Ramakrishna felt he had identified the underlying unity of all religions. His one purpose in life was to visualize God, whom he saw in the feminine aspect. He worshiped her as "the Divine Mother" and talked to her frequently. As Ramakrishna experimented with other religions in the world—the different sects of India and the religions taught by Christ and Muhammad—he concluded that all religions had one feature in common: They were merely different paths to the same God.

One day Sri Ramakrishna was in a very high *samadhi* (state of enlightenment), talking aloud to himself while young Vivekananda was listening attentively. "I have learned a great lesson today," Vivekananda is reported to have said. "If I live, I shall someday give this truth to the world."

What did Vivekananda preach? The ideal objective in life, he said, was service to God and man. A later follower, Swami Prabhavananda, summarized the ideal this way:

When we learn to see God within ourselves, we learn to see Him in all. We learn to see that our own good lies in the good of all Mankind. Thus it is that humanism becomes spiritualized. The ignorant way is to strive to enrich our life on earth and the spiritual way is to try to find out how best we can live on earth in order that we may reach God.[1]

"Thou art That" was the essence of Vedanta, the new movement founded by Vivekananda. In one of his lectures delivered in 1896 in London, entitled "Practical Vedanta," Vivekananda said, "We can do everything. Vedanta teaches men to have faith in themselves first. A

---

[1]Christopher Isherwood, *Vedanta for Modern Man* (New York: Signet Books, 1951), p. 155.

man who does not believe in himself is an atheist. Not believing in the glory of our own soul is what Vedanta calls atheism."[2] That is to say, he considered the human soul to be pure and omniscient and therefore divine.

Swami Vivekananda was the first of the Hindu missionaries to the West to have major popular impact. That was because reincarnation and Eastern philosophy had already become somewhat popular during the nineteenth century, as has been said. During the twentieth century, more teachers arrived from the East to make American disciples. More Western metaphysical societies were formed, many inspired by the Theosophical Society. Reincarnation teaching reached into every level of society. Some of the more influential gurus from the East included Rabindranath Tagore (1861–1941) who wrote the *Gitanjali*; Sri Aurobindo (1872–1950), known for his revolutionary metaphysics, which were explained in a massive three equal volume work, *The Life Divine*; and Ramana Maharishi (1879–1950).

Paramahansa Yogananda (1893–1952) was probably the most influential Eastern teacher in America during the first half of the twentieth century. He first spoke in the United States as India's delegate to an International Congress of Religious Liberals on October 6, 1920, in Boston, Massachusetts. From that time until the day of his death he worked tirelessly to spread the Hindu religion and the teachings of yoga.

He lectured to millions of people across the nation and wrote the immensely popular *Autobiography of a Yogi*, now in its eleventh American edition. That book has been translated into thirteen languages. In 1925 Yogananda founded the Self-Realization Fellowship with in-

---

[2]Clive Johnson, *Vedanta* (New York: Harper & Row Publishers, 1971), p. 188.

ternational headquarters in Los Angeles. SRF is still going strong today. In addition, Yogananda initiated a number of American disciples into the Swami Order, making them gurus in their own right. A number of these have formed organizations of their own and continue to be active.

Edgar Cayce

The American most noted for popularizing reincarnation within the United States was Edgar Cayce. Cayce was born March 18, 1877, on a farm in Hopkinsville, Kentucky. Because of trances and visions he experienced from childhood, Cayce ultimately became known as "the sleeping prophet." He was the leading exponent of "a new world religion" based on immortality of the soul via reincarnation.

Ironically, legend has it that Cayce received a warning about his "gift of vision" when he was a child. One day young Edgar was hunting for a stray cow when he encountered a stranger reading the Bible. The stranger turned out to be Dwight L. Moody, then a Chicago shoe salesman (he had not yet achieved fame as an evangelist). Together they discussed Cayce's strange gift. Moody specifically warned, "You must be very careful to distinguish whether your visions are from God or from Satan." Turning to Leviticus 20:27, Moody read: "A man or a woman who is a medium or a spiritist shall surely be put to death. They shall be stoned with stones, their bloodguiltiness is upon them."

Later, at the age of twenty-one, Cayce was afflicted with a peculiar throat disorder. Entering his familiar "sleep state," he allegedly diagnosed his own problem and effected a cure. Subsequently, using similar trances,

Cayce was able to diagnose and treat many other patients with equal facility. Doctors were amazed.

With only a sixth-grade education, Edgar Cayce astounded the medical profession for some forty-three years. He seemed to have a true power of telepathic readings. Although he had been reared a Christian and even taught Sunday school, he eventually adopted the idea of reincarnation. Then, to support his theory, he reinterpreted the Bible and the teaching of Jesus Christ concerning both resurrection and eternal life.

As a result of his reinterpretation, Cayce considered the life of Jesus of Nazareth to represent only one of thirty previous reincarnations of the same soul. He insisted that Christ was not truly God incarnate, but only another human much like you and me. "All of us," he said, "will eventually achieve perfection by repaying our karmic debt," thus copying the ageless concept of many religions—that each must reap exactly what he sows.

Cayce also insisted that one could continue to identify himself as a Christian and at the same time adopt the concept of reincarnation. He maintained that Christianity and the theory of reincarnation were entirely compatible.[3]

Contradicting the Bible, Cayce went further and claimed that Jesus was actually a sinful soul (Second Corinthians 5:21 states that Christ knew no sin), who had become perfected through numerous reincarnations. "He lived only as a man. He died only as a man."[4]

Cayce said, "Christ is not a man. Jesus was the man, Christ was the messenger . . . Christ in all ages. Jesus

---

[3]Phillip J. Swihart, *Reincarnation, Edgar Cayce and the Bible* (Downers Grove, Ill.: Inter-Varsity Press,1975), pp. 20,24,30.
[4]Jeffrey Furst, ed., *Edgar Cayce's Story of Jesus* (New York: Berkley Publications, 1970), p. 246.

only in one" (Reading 991-1, Edgar Cayce Library). All that, of course, contradicts Hebrews 13:8, which clearly states that Jesus Christ is the same yesterday and today and forever. When Cayce was asked at what time in history Jesus was made aware that He was to be the Savior of the world, Cayce replied, "When He fell, in Eden" (Reading 2067-7), implying that Christ was Adam in reincarnated form.

Gina Cerminara, one of Edgar Cayce's followers, wrote:

For almost twenty centuries the moral sense of the eastern world has been blunted by a theology which teaches the vicarious atonement of sin through Christ, the Son of God . . . [The view that] Christ was the Son of God and that He died for man's salvation . . . has been the great psychological crime because it places responsibility for redemption on something external to the self; it makes salvation dependent on belief in the divinity of another person rather than on self-transformation through belief in one's own intrinsic divinity.[5]

Such a statement epitomizes the crucial difference between reincarnationist beliefs and Christianity.[6]

Cayce also believed that grace is not a gift of God, but is rather the freedom to forgive others and thus save

---

[5]William J. Peterson, *Those Curious New Cults* (New Canaan, Conn.: Keats Publishers, 1973), pp. 43,44.

[6]Taking strong issue with this concept of Christ's diety, C. S. Lewis stated the problem in a different fashion: "A man who is merely a man and said the sort of things that Jesus said would not be a great moral teacher. He would either be a lunatic—on a level with the man who says he is a poached egg—or else he would be the Devil of Hell. You must make your choice. Either this man was, and is, the Son of God; or else a madman or something worse. You can shut Him up for a fool or you can spit on Him or kill Him as a demon; or you can fall at His feet and call Him Lord and God, but let us not come with any patronizing nonsense about His being a great human teacher. He has not left that open to us. He did not intend to." (C.S. Lewis, *Mere Christianity* (New York: Macmillan Company, 1964), p. 56.

ourselves by reducing our karmic debt. According to him, God has already forgiven us all; thus there is no judgment, no eternal accountability, no hell—and also no existence in a place called heaven.

Many considered Cayce a prophet who was given his abilities by some supernatural power. As I reviewed his writings at the headquarters of the Association for Research and Enlightenment in Virginia Beach, Virginia, I had no doubt that Cayce had access to extraordinary and supernatural energies. The question in my mind was, Who or what was the source of his powers? If Cayce's powers were not his own, as he claimed they were not, then they had to have come from an outside source. Were they derived ultimately from God, as he believed, or from Satan, as others have believed?

In addition to being a medium, Cayce also promoted his beliefs in astrology and psychic predictions. Although he claimed to be correct most of the time, his prophecies were not without error. For instance, Cayce correctly predicted the fall of Germany; but at first he had prophesied that Hitler's intentions were good.[7]

Transcendental Meditation

The Eastern guru whose influence is felt the most in the West today is probably Maharishi Mahesh Yogi, founder of Transcendental Meditation. Maharishi Mahesh Yogi, born in India, received a secular education before he studied under a Hindu yogi (or teacher) named Bramananda Saraswati, or Guru Dev. It is said that Guru Dev eventually commissioned Maharishi Mahesh

---

[7]Swihart, p. 50.

Yogi to bring the alleged truths of the transcendental meditation yoga to the West in the 1950s.

Although TM is thought of as a recent development in the West, its principles are not really new. For centuries the art of meditation has been used in Hinduism, Buddhism, and Taoism to escape the "illusory" world in which we live in exchange for the "real" world of the inner self. Early Western converts to the TM movement included, among other well-known personalities, members of the Beatles and, later, of the Beach Boys.

First promoting his movement as religious, Maharishi later tried to secularize it as a "relaxation technique" in an effort to create a plausible image of Hinduism for the Western mind. Claiming to provide "deep rest as a basis for dynamic action," TM says it can help anyone. "Students, housewives, businessmen, scientists, pilots, physicians, musicians, and others have all reported practical benefits in terms of their own needs and aspirations."[8] TM is probably the most Americanized of all the Hindu religious groups operating in this country, with thirty thousand or more initiates per month and now claiming close to a million Americans.[9]

The core of TM teaching is the *mantra*, a supposedly meaningless, one-syllable sound that one utters while meditating to achieve a state of "relaxed awareness." Unknown to many people, the *mantra* is actually one of many Sanskrit words of divine worship used for communication with the Hindu deities.

The usual TM initiate is invited into an incense-filled room containing an altar. Kneeling, he fixes his gaze on a

---

[8]"Transcendental Meditation as Taught by Maharishi Mahesh Yogi," SIMS-IMS National Center, 1015 Gaylet Ave., Los Angeles, 1973, p. 2.
[9]Jack Sparks, *The Mind Benders* (Nashville: Thomas Nelson, Inc., 1977), pp. 45–49.

picture of Guru Dev, predecessor of the Maharishi, while someone else in the room sings the hymn of worship called the *puja*, the initiation liturgy. Since the puja is in Sanskrit, the initiate does not understand what is being sung.

After the ceremony the initiate is given a personal mantra, intended to be a private key to unlock the gates of meditation into "bliss-consciousness."

While TM proponents continue to claim that their meditation is not religious, many meditators do come to accept Maharishi's Hindu doctrine of reincarnation. Thus reincarnation is propagated under the guise of something as simple and appealing as relaxation!

Krishna Consciousness

Several years ago I encountered a strange group of young people wrapped in orange robes and coming out of a hotel in New York City. Walking barefoot in winter weather, heads shaved except for an isolated ponytail, they were chanting *Hare, Krishna/ Hare, Krishna/ Krishna, Krishna/ Hare, Hare/ Hare, Rama/ Hare, Rama/ Rama, Rama/ Hare, Hare.* One of them asked if I would like to buy some incense. Meanwhile, the others were dancing and chanting with a distant, distracted expression on their faces.

I learned later that these were devotees of Krishna consciousness, an Americanized import based on a fifteenth-century sect of Hinduism dedicated to the worship of Lord Krishna. Krishna was said by his followers to be the ultimate incarnation of god as man. Although traditional Hinduism cites Lord Krishna (one of the principal characters in the Bhagavad-Gita) as the seventh incarnation of the god Vishnu, the followers of

Krishna claim that this is not so: Krishna himself, they say, is the Supreme God, and one of his other names is Vishnu.

A. C. Bhaktivedanta Swami Prabhupada came to New York City in 1965 and founded the International Society for Krishna Consciousness (abbreviated ISKCON) a year later. His followers, called Hare Krishnas, were once easily recognized by their distinctive dress, shaved heads (the ponytail was said to serve as a handle by which Lord Krishna could snatch them up to heaven), and their street chanting. The Hare Krishna chant, if precisely repeated, is said to produce spiritual benefits even if the chanters or the listeners are not devotees. The purpose of the chant, summarized by a phrase abstracted from the Bhagavad-Gita, was taught by Bhaktivedanta: "When your mind is no longer disturbed by the flowery language of the Vedas and when it remains fixed in the trance of self-realization, then you will have attained the divine consciousness" (Text 56, verse 53). In recent years, possibly to gain respectability and acceptance, many U.S. converts have donned Western apparel, cut off their ponytails, and reserved chanting for times of worship.

The twofold goals of the Hare Krishna movement are to glorify Krishna to the world and to convert the world to Krishna. Although Krishna is said to have been incarnated in somewhat the same way as was Jesus Christ, the Hare Krishnas do not think of Krishna as Christ. To them he is a personal god interested in their welfare whom they therefore desire to please. Jesus Christ, they say, was a good man, perhaps even a prophet, or a son of God in the sense that we all are sons of God. But Jesus Christ is not considered to be an avatar (an incarnation of a deity).

Although claiming to be in harmony with Christianity, ISKCON actually believes that it is the only true religion and that the path to salvation through chanting the Hare Krishna mantra is the ultimate path. As universalists and reincarnationists, ISKCON adherents believe that eventually even Christians will be liberated from this false world of illusion and then will be able to appreciate the great Lord Krishna.

ISKCON devotees follow exacting rules of conduct, are vegetarians, and have a strict sexual code. Nonetheless, Krishna is said to be a "fun-loving" god with over sixteen thousand wives. Although accounts of his life refer to many acts of violence, he is nevertheless said to be sinless, an immunity conferred on gods only:

. . . the violation of religious laws by the gods and the daring acts of the glorious do not bring any stains, as fire is not stained by feeding on impure substances. But those that are not gods should never commit such deeds, even in thought. If a man foolishly drinks poison in imitation of Siva, he is sure to die. The words of the gods are true, but their acts are sometimes true and sometimes not.[10]

Out of curiosity I asked one follower why meditation and worship were so important. He stated that meditation and worship drew them nearer to Krishna. When pressed, he admitted that meditation did not solve anyone's problems, but it did make a person feel a lot better. I learned something else about Krishna. This playful supergod could be worshiped in the form of any idol since he is thought to be present in everything, everywhere.[11]

---

[10]Walter Martin, ed., *The New Cults* (Santa Ana, Calif.: Vision House, 1980), p. 84.
[11]Sparks, pp. 96,97.

I wondered why American young people would be attracted to a religion so spiritually and culturally foreign. Later I learned that people like ex-Beatle George Harrison (who wrote about Krishna in "My Sweet Lord") contributed generously to the support of ISKCON. Such songs, of course, not only revealed what former members of the Beatles believed, but also influenced their fans. Perhaps the attraction of so "human" a god as Krishna and the possibility of self-salvation also appealed to some.

The Church of Scientology

Encouraged by the permissiveness and experimentation of the sixties counterculture, an enormous number of new religious movements have developed in America in the last fifteen years. Many of them are Western revivals of traditional Eastern sects. These teach yoga, meditation, and a theory of reincarnation that is consistent with classical Hinduism and Buddhism. Others are mixtures of Eastern philosophy and Western occultism. These groups try to take the best of all the mystical religions in order to speed up the process of enlightenment. There is often a greater preoccupation with reincarnation in these groups than in offshoots of the classic Eastern religions. Still others are brand-new inventions of people who claim to have discovered new spiritual truths. Many times these individuals will say that these new discoveries are, in fact, the most ancient spiritual truths, lost for many thousands of years until their current rediscovery.

So many new religious groups are in existence today that it would be impossible to list them all here. But a look at one invented in our day illustrates how exotic a reincarnation teaching can become. The group I have in mind is the Church of Scientology.

L. Ron Hubbard, a former science fiction writer and founder of Scientology, teaches that millions and millions of years ago all that existed were free and boundless spiritual entities called Thetans. For amusement, the Thetans created a Matter/Energy/Space/Time (MEST) universe to play in. They descended into the universe they had made and assumed various physical forms. After a while, they became so enthralled with their game that they took it to be real. They identified with the bodies they had taken and became trapped in them.

According to Scientology, this story describes the origin of life in the universe, not only on earth, but throughout all the galaxies. Because the Thetans had forgotten their original identity, they were doomed to migrate from body to body, all over the universe, whenever the physical form they were inhabiting at the time died.

The aim of Scientology is first to clear a person of the attachment produced by millions of past-life experiences, and then to teach him or her to become an Operating Thetan (OT) once again.

One of the most secret reincarnation stories in Scientology is meant for the eyes of OT-III's only (III is one of the highest levels of Operating Thetans). It is said to be designed to kill anyone who reads it without proper preparation. The story concerns a malicious character named Xenn, a tyrant in some confederation of planets 75 million years ago. Xenn tried to control his population by fusing it together. He dumped the poor creatures on volcanoes, then dropped hydrogen bombs on them. This gave them the false impression that they were one. Fused and confused, they were further deceived by iconic representations of angels and devils. Today, everybody is made up of these disoriented souls. But

OT-III Scientologists are the only ones who know this. They alone can save the world.[12]

The general teaching on reincarnation within Scientology is just as bizarre as its esoteric doctrine. It is said, for example, that humans cry salt tears because of their previous existence as oysters that had grains of sand lodged in their shells.

Zen Buddhism

Zen is a branch of Buddhism that has gained many converts in the West. More properly described as a mental discipline than a religious practice, Zen is a kind of systemized existentialism. All truth is to be found within the essence of what is, and all of existence is relevant only in the instant of its perception in the here and now.

The goal of Zen is to arrive intuitively at the enlightened mind which has been cleared of conceptual clutter. This mind (called "*bodhi* mind") supposedly is able to see reality as it is instead of through the filter of human concepts about reality. In Zen, there is no perception of a need for salvation, only a need for realization, or *satori*.

Since its development around 500 B.C., Zen Buddhism has emphasized meditation (called *zazen*) as the means to achieve enlightenment. The word *Zen* means "insight," and this insight is gained by paying bare attention to one's breath during meditation, allowing all thoughts and concepts to drift away. Zen is very popular in Japan and has also gained a strong following in the United States. Its teachings do not address the concept of reincarnation, since any notions of an afterlife would only distract from one's bare attention to the here and now.

---

[12]*The Real Paper* (Cambridge, Mass.), December 8, 1979.

Satanism

When Anton LaVey played the role of Satan in the 1968 film, *Rosemary's Baby*, his personal philosophy was not generally known. A year later LaVey wrote in *The Satanic Bible:* "Lucifer is risen, once more to proclaim: 'This is the age of Satan. Satan rules the earth.' "[13]

That statement echoed the closing scene of the movie, in which the evil witch leader, Castavet, announces:

> *God is dead!*
> *God is dead and Satan lives.*
> *The year is One, the first year of our Lord!*
> *The year is One.*
> *God is done.*

Ever since LaVey, the "black pope," formed his church of Satan in San Francisco in 1966, Satanism has resurged as a religion in America, even in its infancy claiming more than fifteen thousand members. Devils, demons, and witches have made the greatest comeback since the Middle Ages. Satanism is a continuing fad in movies, television, and other entertainment media, appealing to people's appetites for the sensational, the bizarre, and the macabre. Following the "harmless" television programs "Dark Shadows" and "Bewitched" came William Blatty's *The Exorcist, Omen I, Omen II,* and now *Omen III: The Final Conflict, The Other, The Amityville Horror,* and *The Scanners.* Others are on the drawing boards, aiming to capitalize on the current craving for occultic knowledge and scary experiences.

---

[13]Anton S. LaVey, *The Satanic Bible* (New York: Avon Books, 1969), p. 23.

More than three hundred thousand copies of *The Satanic Bible* are claimed to be in circulation in America alone. Satanists believe that humanity is inherently selfish, sensual, and violent, and that these attributes should be encouraged and celebrated. They maintain that people are free to do whatever they wish, free to perform any sin, free to live for fulfillment of their desires.

Like most cultic groups, Satanists believe in some form of reincarnation and teach that human beings control their own destiny.[14]

It Can Happen Here

Reincarnation has become the most popular Eastern religious concept now evident in the Western world. Some sixty percent of the American people are said to believe in the possibility of reincarnation. Cult expert Walter Martin, noting that the idea of reincarnation is a basic belief in the world of the occult, has said, "It's important to remember that reincarnation is connected extensively and almost exclusively with the world of the occult."[15] If we believe one of these concepts, we may soon find ourselves involved with the other.

---

[14]Leon McBeth, *Strange New Religions* (Nashville: Broadman Press, 1977), p. 113.

[15]Walter Martin, *The Riddle of Reincarnation* (Santa Ana, Calif.: Vision House Publishers, Inc., 1977), p. 15.

CHAPTER 5

THE GOSPEL ACCORDING TO REINCARNATION

What does reincarnation offer? What is its message? Using five major topics as a base, I would like to answer those questions. At the same time I will attempt to compare reincarnation and Christianity on some significant issues related to this discussion.

I. Vision for the World

It is important to understand that reincarnation seeks to address the matter of one's *inner* life. The philosophy deals only with the person, not with his or her environment. Although it offers some promise for personal improvement, it makes no provision for the "real" world.

In India, for instance, rats are permitted to consume hundreds of tons of food each year while human beings starve. Yet rats must not be killed; they might be one's own relatives. They are considered important, too, even if they are "less equal" than some others in the caste system.

But even that kind of importance makes little difference, since nothing is really "real." The world itself is "unreal," as defined by the word *maya*. Hinduism declares that the world actually doesn't exist at all, except in our minds. The Hindu gods are not concerned about matters external to the self. It is unimportant that the world, which "doesn't exist," may be about to kill us through famines, floods, hurricanes, and earthquakes (which don't exist either).

Christianity, in contrast to the reincarnation faiths, deals directly with the world "out there." God, who created all things, controls not only the individual but the world, the universe, and everything that exists. Further, He cares about all things. He deals not only with the *inner* life but with the *outer* world. Everything is in His hands.

Christianity, therefore, is both a personal and an others-oriented religion, concerned with personal salvation and also with outreach to the world—especially in personal relationships. Followers are to love God and then "love thy neighbor as thyself." Alleviating suffering and demonstrating practical concern for others are strong priorities for Christians, because they care about others' inner lives as well as their own.

Meanwhile, reincarnation in its world view (or lack of it) runs into an interesting demographic problem. Reincarnation falters as the population explodes. If, as claimed by most reincarnationists, human souls are not created but have existed forever and all began their spiritual journey to God-consciousness at the same time, then no new souls are being created for the increasing number of bodies now populating the earth.[1] If that is so, how could the "birthing cycle" of self-replacement develop into a population explosion?

The world continues to show a geometric increase in its population, with the time required for the population's doubling now taking less than one generation.

---

[1]Sir Norman Anderson, ed., *The World's Religions*, Vol. 1 (Grand Rapids: Eerdmans, 1976), pp. 138–42.

World population was approaching 4.7 billion in 1980 and was predicted to double again in ten years. According to the concept of reincarnation, the population of the world should not only remain constant, as people exchange bodies at death, but should be *decreasing*, as some lucky souls vacate the scene for nirvana. Admitting that the population is increasing, some modern reincarnationists have tried to say that new souls are being added from other planets, perhaps arriving like UFOs.

In other words, if no new souls are being created and old souls are continually being absorbed back into Brahma, then the population should be receding. But just the opposite is true. More persons are alive now than have ever existed in all of history before. The ancient creators of reincarnation had no way of foreseeing that there wouldn't be enough souls to go around to fill all the extra bodies that eventually would appear in the world.

According to Dr. Robert Morey, transmigrationists offer a partial answer.[2] They believe that the necessary human souls can be transferred from the insect and animal world to human form. But if that theory is true, the population of those lower creatures should be decreasing as a result of that unforeseen shift into human souls. There is no data to substantiate this trend.

Many Western reincarnationists prefer not to believe in the transmigration of souls from human to animal bodies. It's distasteful. As a result, they can offer no plausible explanation for the increased population without proposing some new theory to explain securing enough souls to fill those bodies. On this issue, reincarnation becomes self-indicting.

---

[2]Robert A. Morey, *Reincarnation and Christianity* (Minneapolis: Bethany Fellowship, 1980), p. 38.

II. Karmic Debt/Forgiveness of Sins

According to reincarnation, you must undo all wrong-doing incurred in any of your lives—you cannot be forgiven. You therefore undergo cyclic rebirth into new bodily existences and suffer now because of the past.

Supposedly this explains why people have physical and mental imperfections. They have committed bad deeds in a previous life. (As has been said earlier, "bad deeds" means living as if this world is real instead of seeking nirvana through meditation and other practices.) That is to say, what you do is what you get—in the next life. No one else can pay your karmic debt for you; you are personally responsible; there is no escape from your karma. All of the suffering experienced in this life is something you must endure as a result of acts in a previous life. No one can interfere; even the Hindu gods cannot alter the course of karma.

In sharp contrast, Christian theology boldly cuts across all theories of karma. Isaiah 64:6 says that all our righteousness is like a filthy rag (see also Prov. 14:12; Eph. 2:8; Titus 3:5). We can never be exonerated of past wrongs by performing works of righteousness. Christianity meets this problem of sin and guilt head-on. We are told in Hebrews 1:1–3 that Jesus Christ already has made the total payment for sin—for *all* "karmic" debts, one might say. God the Father appointed His Son:

. . . heir of all things, by whom also he made the worlds; who being the brightness of his glory, and the express image of his person, and upholding all things by the word of his power, when he had by himself purged our sins, sat down on the right hand of the Majesty on high (vv. 2,3 KJV).

The word *purge* comes from a Greek word that means "to cleanse." From this same source we get our word for *purgative* or *cathartic*. The verse here means that Jesus Christ, by His sacrifice, purged or cleansed away our sins forever.

Therefore, it is not necessary for you and me to pass through cycles of rebirth. We are told in Hebrews 9:12 that Christ entered *once* into the Holy Place, "having obtained eternal redemption." The thought is continued in verse 14: "how much more will the blood of Christ, who through the eternal Spirit offered Himself without blemish to God, cleanse your conscience from dead works to serve the living God?" This is further emphasized in the next chapter: "He, having offered *one sacrifice for sins for all time*, sat down at the right hand of God . . . For by *one offering* He has perfected for all time those who are sanctified" (Heb. 10:12,14, italics mine).

Reincarnation blatantly denies the atonement of Jesus Christ. If you belong to reincarnation, *you* pay the price. If you belong to Christ, *He* paid the price for your sins *forever*. The meat of the question for you and me is this: *Do we want karma or do we want Christ and the forgiveness He offers?*

This issue of forgiveness ties in with the issue of a world view. Since according to the law of karma each individual life has no purpose except to suffer retribution for its own misdeeds, reincarnation offers no concept of living for the good of others or for the glory of God. One does not even live for the glory of self. If you ever reach nirvana you immediately lose your identity and achieve "supreme nothingness" in a god that is everywhere. Oblivion.

Dr. Morey believes that the law of karma robs history of meaning—when everything is repeated endlessly.

It teaches that suffering is the only real purpose in life . . . intrinsically selfish and self-centered, it cripples the unity of humanity since each soul is trapped in a cycle of rebirths which benefits only that individual soul. It produces despair, fatalism, pessimism, etc. . . . It is a psychologically devastating concept. It causes people to ignore the suffering of others. It does not encourage people to alleviate human suffering. It produces pride among the rich and healthy and shame within the poor and sick . . . it allows no place for forgiveness since karma can neither give nor recognize forgiveness. How can the law of karma be *just* if it makes repentance useless?[3]

III. Human Nature

Closely related to a view of forgiveness, of course, is one's view of human nature. How does reincarnation explain our moral situation? Humankind appears to be as wicked today as ever, and more so. Reincarnationists (and even humanists) must agree that people have not improved significantly through the centuries. Witness the increase in crime, murder, immorality, and depravity in the world.

Yet reincarnationist doctrines postulate that humanity should be demonstrating progressive improvement, as a result of the karmic suffering paid through multiple lives. We should notice humankind becoming better and better instead of worse and worse.

Look at today's society. Are you afraid to go out at night? Were you ten years ago? Why are the sales of burglar alarms and special door locks booming?

Or is the premise of Christianity correct? Human beings are basically and unquestionably evil when left to their own devices.

---

[3]Ibid., pp. 41,42.

Another important concept of reincarnation is that the poor deserve their suffering while the rich deserve the "good life." Yet those who believe in transmigration perpetuate much of the starvation and famines in India and in parts of Asia. They refuse to kill rodents that deplete large segments of the food supplies, and they refuse to stop the spread of disease by insect control.

Many Westerners who believe in reincarnation have rejected the idea of transmigration by limiting reincarnation to humans. This Western version seems benign enough; even some church people have come to accept reincarnation, perhaps in an attempt to do as they please and to please God, too. After all, who wants to face the prospect of hell in another world for sins committed here, if one can select a "time payment plan" and live a holy life later in the familiarity of the same world? But in reality we have no such choice.

One soon sees some possible reasons for the convenient deviations of reincarnation from the original concept. People are attempting to encompass the best of all religions. After all, what could be more open-minded—and palatable—than to accept all people and all faiths? The danger is subtle. It is the path to worship the god within: self. This new form of reincarnation further underlines our imperfect, sinful human nature.

IV. Past Lives, Hypnosis, and ESP

If reincarnation is true, then all of us have past lives. Can we remember them? Can we look back in time and see ourselves as we were before? Trying to find the answers to such questions is tempting, so tempting that hypnosis and ESP have become closely associated with reincarnation thought as a means to explore our "former selves."

The use of hypnosis and ESP has steadily gained a degree of credibility in parts of the scientific world. Yet many case studies have not proved credible with time. (How many Jesuses, Buddhas, Moseses, or Muhammads could there have been?)

Then there are cases like the one described in the book *The Search for Bridey Murphy*. The story, as was briefly mentioned earlier, concerns a woman who, under hypnosis, was taken back to early nineteenth-century Ireland. She described clearly the coastline where she lived, customs, clothing—all in the ancient Gaelic language, the same language she had spoken in her alleged previous life. She claimed that her name in that life was Bridey Murphy.

Later, some investigators discovered that this woman had spent her early years in the company of her grandmother, who had used history books to teach her about old Ireland and who spoke in Gaelic to the child. As the child grew older, she forgot the language and the history books with her conscious mind, but the experiences were retained deep in her memory. The investigators believed that under hypnosis she was able to recall some of the events she had learned as a child, as well as the Gaelic language of her grandmother. Other investigators claimed that years earlier an old Irishwoman had lived across the street from the hypnotized woman and that she was the source of what the woman recalled.[4] Nevertheless, the book about the "discovery" of Bridey Murphy was published and touted at the time as absolute proof of reincarnation.[5]

---

[4] Kenneth L. Woodward, "Do We Live More Than Once?" *McCall's* 106:28, June 1979, p. 128.

[5] Walter R. Martin, *The Riddle of Reincarnation* (Santa Ana, Calif.: Vision House, 1979).

What about déjà vu? Most of us have such impressions at one time or another. As said earlier, reincarnationists often use this phenomenon as proof that people indeed experience recall from past lives.

Many explanations of déjà vu have been proposed. The sense of association may arise, for instance, as the subconscious mind tries to recall some experience from youth. We may see a person who looks very much like someone we have previously known. We may visit a place we "feel" we've been to before. The subconscious mind relates the present instance to a previous event that the conscious mind does not remember. Also, researchers have documented a possible physiological basis for déjà vu. Impressions are sometimes delayed for a fraction of a second, in the transmittal from the eye or ear to the brain, so that the conscious mind "feels" that it has seen or heard the experience before.

Rarely, recall associations relate to identification projections. Such may have been the case when Mark David Chapman pathologically identified himself as John Lennon, disposing of the imposter (the real John Lennon) in a barrage of bullets. Identification with admired historic figures is a common pathological finding among patients on psychiatric wards. At least ten percent of psychotics consider themselves to be Jesus Christ, Napoleon, or some other important historical figure.

Past-life recall through hypnotic regression may actually be a form of occultic communication. Such suspended states of the mind have been self-induced for centuries by mediums and witches as they invite spirit control from metaphysical forces.

The Scriptures never suggest that occultic practices are unreal, but rather imply their demonic origin. Any apparent results are not from God, because God forbids any dabbling in the world of the occult (see Ex. 22:18;

Lev. 19:31; 20:6,27; Is. 47:12–15). Deuteronomy 13:1–3 sums it up:

"If a prophet or a dreamer of dreams arises among you and gives you a sign or a wonder, and the sign or the wonder comes true, concerning which he spoke to you, saying, 'Let us go after other gods (whom you have not known) and let us serve them,' you shall not listen to the words of that prophet or that dreamer of dreams; for the LORD your God is testing you to find out if you love the LORD your God with all your heart and with all your soul."

But, you might say, surely ESP and past recall are not an invitation to serve "other gods." Surely, they're harmless. The Bible tells of a girl who had the "spirit of divination" (ESP?) in Acts 16:16–18. She was possessed with an ability to make uncannily accurate forecasts; at least it was sufficiently accurate to be profitable for her masters. Irritated by her remarks after many days, Paul said to the spirit in her (notice he did not address the girl herself): " 'I command you in the name of Jesus Christ to come out of her!' " (v. 18). And the demonic spirit "came out at that very moment." When her owners realized that she had lost her psychic ability, they became so infuriated that they had Paul and Silas beaten with rods and thrown into jail (see Acts 16:19–24).

Without realizing the danger, many people dabble in hypnosis or past-lives recall, unaware of the potential, underlying spiritual reality of satanic evil. They are unaware that they are playing with fire, as were some young men in the Book of Acts who tried doing exorcisms without God's protection. " 'I recognize Jesus, and I know about Paul, but who are you?' " asked the evil spirit within the man. Then the man with the spirit leaped on the experimenters and beat them up, so that they fled naked and wounded into the streets (see Acts 19:13–16).

Horoscopes and fortune-telling, too, often serve as seemingly benign invitations to the fringes of the mystic world where subsequent introductions to occult forces may follow. Even children's Ouija boards can lead to serious problems. Back in the 1930s a wise Christian thinker wrote this in his autobiography:

My brother and I used to play with . . . the Ouija board; but we were among the few, I imagine, who played in a mere spirit of play. Nevertheless I would not altogether rule out the suggestion of some that we were playing with fire, or even with hell-fire. In the words that were written for us, there was nothing ostensibly degrading, but any amount that was deceiving. I saw quite enough of the thing to be able to testify, with complete certainty, that something happens which is not in the ordinary sense natural, or produced by the normal and conscious human will. Whether it is produced by some subconscious but still human force, or by some powers, good, bad or indifferent, which are external to humanity, I would not myself attempt to decide. The only thing I will say with complete confidence, about that mystic and invisible power, is that it tells lies. The lies may be larks or they may be lures to the imperilled soul or they may be a thousand other things; but whatever they are, they are not truths about the other world; or for that matter about this world.[6]

Still, some of us try to deny that these "innocent" pastimes involve supernatural, evil forces that are real, capable of killing, disfiguring, or forever possessing the minds and bodies of participants.

One day I was on call at the clinic, having seen Mr. F. in the emergency room the week before. At that time he was a nervous wreck, complaining of many symptoms, but with distinct psychosomatic problems. The following is taken from his case history.

---

[6]G.K. Chesterton, *The Autobiography of G.K. Chesterton* (New York: Sheed & Ward, 1936), p. 77.

Mr. F. had seen palm readers in the past, had joined a group devoted to self-improvement through self-realization by analyzing one another's past lives. Seances were found helpful at first, but then the real troubles started for Mr. F. The spirit guides would visit him at home. Then they visited him at work. Concentration became difficult. His work showed forgetfulness. One task would remain unfinished as he compulsively started another. His wife became alienated and neglected. He was afraid to sleep because the voices continually were giving him instructions.

This week Mr. F. had just slashed his wrists with a razor and was bleeding profusely. When I saw him, he was pale, and blood was all over his clothes. The nurse was trying to control the bleeding, holding the wounds tightly with a towel. Now and then, whenever the nurse shifted position, a small pumping stream of blood would jet into the air from a severed radial artery. A Kelly clamp controlled the bleeding until we could suture the artery.

Here was a case of demonic control good enough for a movie production. Starting innocently enough with past-recall therapy, it had mushroomed into a suicide attempt. Mr. F. said he had found no other way to escape the voices. The spirit forces were so real and his fear so extreme that he preferred to take his life.

I was delighted to tell him that there is another side to the spirit world, of which he was apparently unaware. Now he is no longer a student of the occult, but a follower of Christ. The "Jesus-connection" freed him.

I saw a two-hour TV special called "Death, the Ultimate Mystery" by Sandler Films, Inc. The theme of the picture was life after death, and the relevant concepts of each world religion on this subject were presented. It ended with reincarnation being vividly and convincingly presented.

The scene at the end presented one woman who through hypnotic regression began speaking about her supposed past lives. She recalled living as a little girl in Canton, Ohio. She had died at an early age, trampled underfoot by runaway horses pulling a carriage down Main Street. Subsequent research revealed that this street had indeed existed in the mid-1800s. A candy store she described had existed on the street corner she named. The names of several people she remembered as living at that time were verified.

Assuming that all of those findings were correct, we have at least four choices to explain this phenomenon:

1. She really lived at that time and has been reincarnated.

2. The hypnosis in some way unearthed a long-forgotten experience from her youth buried in the subconscious mind. (She may have read a book or seen a movie about Canton, Ohio).

3. The whole thing is pure coincidence.

4. A satanic emissary revealed to her things that happened in the mid-1800s in Canton, Ohio, making her believe she was there.

My own conclusion, after reviewing many similar cases, is that the fourth explanation is most likely.

Christians have no excuse to be gullible. We have been specifically instructed by the apostle John how to discern which information from the spirit world is true and which is false:

Beloved, do not believe every spirit, but test the spirits to see whether they are from God. . . . By this you know the Spirit of God: every spirit that confesses that Jesus Christ has come in the flesh is from God; and every spirit that does not confess Jesus is not from God; and this is the spirit of the antichrist, of which you have heard that it is coming, and now it is already in the world (1 John 4:1–3).

The spirit of the antichrist is already in the world. How do we test to see if the spirit is the antichrist's?

John told us how: If anyone denies that Jesus is the Christ (the Anointed One), he is of the antichrist (see 1 John 2:22,23). Most reincarnationists flatly deny that Jesus is the Son of God. When was the last time you read about someone under hypnosis or using ESP acclaiming Jesus? Do you believe in reincarnation? Are you responding to the spirit of antichrist?

V. The Matter of the Occult

Reincarnationists often deny that they have any association with the occult. Rather, they may claim to have a more scientific belief than Christians. Back in the 1950s, Christopher Isherwood wrote:

. . . spiritism, astrology, clairvoyance, mental healing and the study of the occult symbolism now preoccupy hundreds of thousands of people. Such studies are often founded upon ancient Hindu lore—the practice of astrology, for example, is still very popular in India—and they tend to be surrounded by an atmosphere of 'oriental mystery.' But they have nothing whatever to do with the aims of Vedanta.[7]

On the contrary, there is firm evidence that occultic and mystic forces are inextricably bound to reincarnation. The use of those forces to "prove" reincarnation is found in nearly all the writings of popular reincarnationists. For instance, Hans Holzer used a Ouija board.[8] Edgar Cayce was a self-admitted medium through whom spirits spoke. In Jess Stearn's writings we find the use of astrology, mediums, and spirit guides.[9] Without the use

---

[7]Christopher Isherwood, *Vedanta for Modern Man* (New York: Signet Books, 1951), p. 12.

[8]Hans Holzer, *Born Again* (New York: Doubleday & Company, Inc., 1976), p. 73.

of occultic automatic writing, there would not be any reincarnation books by Ruth Montgomery on the market.[10] Nor would there be the bizarre conclusions and practices of a pioneer physician researcher in the field of death and dying, who has now come to rely on the assistance of "spirit guides."[11]

God denounces such practices as "abominable" and "detestable." In a most unyielding tone God said:

> There shalt not be found among you any one that . . . useth divination [fortune-tellers, palm readers, soothsayers],
>> or an observer of times [psychics, astrologers, past-lives therapists]
>> or an enchanter [one who uses hypnosis or casts spells]
>> or a witch [followers of Satan],
>> or a charmer [one who uses Ouija boards, Tarot cards, pendulums, automatic writing, good luck pieces],
>> or a consulter with familiar spirits [mediums, spirit guides, yoga, ESP, and psychic phenomena]
>> or a wizard [sorcerers]
>> or a necromancer [one who uses seances or calls up the dead] (Deut. 18:10–12 KJV).

Those arts are evil. God says they are not from Him (see Is. 8:19,20). But they are powerful, nevertheless, and of satanic origin. Are modern psychic predictions unerringly correct? No, they are frequently wrong. Why? God says He can frustrate such people, make fools out of diviners, and make the knowledge of supposedly wise individuals be absurd (see Is. 44:25).

This confusion among diviners and psychics is not new (see Mic. 3:7). Over two thousand years ago, Hananiah

---

[9]Jess Stearn, *The Search for a Soul* (New York: Doubleday & Company, Inc., 1973), p. 152.

[10]Ruth Montgomery, *Here and Hereafter* (New York: Coward-McCann and George Hegan, Inc., 1968). See also *A World Beyond* and *Companions Along the Way.*

[11]*People* Weekly Magazine, October 29, 1979, p. 30.

gave the Jewish people a prediction that was not from God, causing them to trust in a lie. In this case God didn't merely confuse Hananiah. He caused him to die (see Jer. 28:16,17).

Something for Everyone

Hell is not a popular subject. Yet, its existence and purpose are accepted by those who hold to true, orthodox Christianity. The Hindu concept of reincarnation is a more palatable doctrine to many, one with which many spiritist faiths have become enamored: Scientology, Theosophy, Eckankar, Spiritualism, the Self-Realization Fellowship, and so on.

Those faiths claim that people return to this world, a place they already know. As one student put it, "Why worry about hell when you can choose no judgment at all? It's a person's conscience that creates his reality. By our will we select our genetics, our parents, our environment, and our social standing. To change our circumstances we merely need to change our minds. Everything is a continuum. Things and thoughts and energy are merely different points on the same vista. And today the mystic and the scientist are becoming one, seeking the same answer."

Perhaps his comments reveal why so many people have turned to religious outlooks that claim to represent the best of all religions combined into one, with reincarnation as a base.

"Aren't we all brothers under the skin?" one guru asked during an interview he granted me following a service at his ashram. "All religions really worship the same god. You call him one thing, and I call him another. So you see, you can keep your Christian faith when you join our group because our god is really your God."

Imagine, I said to myself, *this guru offers me a religion with no sin, no hell, no judgment. I just find myself. After all, he said that god is not only in me, I am god! Besides, he tells me I won't lose my Christian identity. It's like having my cake and eating it too.*

Which view is right in this struggle between Christianity and reincarnation? Christ claims that He is God and that salvation occurs through none other but Him. The reincarnation faiths discard that teaching, saying that self-realization replaces it. These views are incompatible. Each claims exclusivity of doctrine.

The Christian world view is in sharp contrast to the Hindu world view. In Christianity Jesus Christ is the only Savior and the only Son of God (see John 1:14; Acts 4:12). In Christianity we have knowledge of God, His will, and the world around us—through the objective and concise record of the Bible and through the incarnation of God's Son (see Heb. 1:1–3). In Christianity, salvation insures eternal peace with God and fellowship with our Creator (see Rev. 21:3,4).

By contrast, in Hinduism a person becomes his or her own savior (after numerous rebirths); Jesus was supposedly only one of many manifestations of God; knowledge of god is not objective but is achieved through spiritual or physical exercise (yoga) designed to rid one of karma so that the individual can experience the presence of god; salvation results in losing one's own identity by becoming "one" with the all-encompassing deity.

In summary, Hindu enlightenment comes from existential and mystical inner perception, realization, or intuition. In the Christian Bible we have a continuous, nonconflicting record of God's dealings with humankind. Hindu writings, by comparison, are varied and contradictory, making evident their development by finite thinkers over thousands of years.

Realization of one's own impersonal part in the cosmic mind is the goal of Hindu yoga. That goal is expressed in the following beautiful phrases of the Upanishads, part of the Hindu Vedas, which advocate worshiping many gods and goddesses through the self:

Know that the Self is the rider and the body the chariot, that the intellect is the charioteer, and the mind of the reins . . . he who lacks discrimination, whose mind is unsteady and whose heart is impure, never reaches the goal, but is born again and again, but he who has discrimination, whose mind is steady and whose heart is pure, reaches the goal and having reached it is born no more.

The man who has a sound understanding for the charioteer, a controlled mind for the reins—he it is that reaches the end of the journey, the supreme abode of Vishnu, the all-pervading (*Katha*, Vol. I, iii, 3-9,12-15).

Modern religions incorporating reincarnation have tried to bridge the gap to Christianity, especially as relates to the problem of the afterlife. This transition is not a subject one can dismiss lightly and still claim allegiance to the teachings of Jesus Christ.

CHAPTER 6

DOES THE SUPERNATURAL REALLY EXIST?

Is there any way we can find that strange dimension the spirit world, the abode of God—that place called *eternity?* The question has plagued humankind through the centuries. Thousands of years ago Job asked, "Can you discover the depths of God? Can you discover the limits of the Almighty?" (Job 11:7).

Reincarnationists say we look *within* ourselves to find God. The Scriptures teach that we look *outside* ourselves to find God (see Rom. 1:20). Of all the gods worshiped in the world today, only One has identified Himself by visiting the earth in human form. That One is the God who revealed Himself in Jesus Christ. "God, after He spoke long ago to the fathers in the prophets in many portions and in many ways, in these last days has spoken to us in His Son . . ." (Heb. 1:1,2).

Reincarnationists claim that all of us living in this world are beings from the spirit world, existing in reincarnated form and making the transition from previous lives to ultimate perfection: oneness with God. Nowadays almost everybody seems to be voting for a spirit world's existence. Hollywood and television are sensationalizing the spirit world with various productions about the macabre and the supernatural. Hollywood is a little late. The Scriptures have always taught that each of us has an inborn awareness of this spirit world. What the apostle Paul said almost two thousand years ago is still true today:

That which is known about God is evident within them; for God made it evident to them. For since the creation of the world His invisible attributes, His eternal power and divine nature, have been clearly seen, being understood through what has been made, so that they are without excuse (Rom. 1:19,20).

Centuries before that, the psalmist similarly reminded human beings of the evidence for the existence of God:

The heavens are telling of the glory of God;
And their expanse is declaring the work of His hands.
Day to day pours forth speech,
And night to night reveals knowledge (Ps. 19:1,2).

Evidence from Astronomy?

For centuries the Bible has said that the spirit world—eternity—exists. Now, science is discovering that too. Astronomers (not to be confused with astrologers) have found "black holes" in galaxies similar to our Milky Way. The Milky Way is thought to have at least one black hole, a collapsed star whose gravitational force is so strong that it cannot even emit its own light. At this moment, astronomers say, this star is drawing in other stars near it like a vacuum cleaner and growing in mass and size. One day it will explode and shake the heavens. Can you believe that?

As theorized in a movie called *The Black Hole*, should some spaceship become caught in the orbit of one of these black hole phenomena, the gravitational force would be great enough to pull the spaceship in at the speed of light. According to Einstein's theory of relativity, the occupants of the spaceship would at that point enter eternity, never hearing the next tick of the clock, never again seeing the clock move forward, never changing. The spaceship's crew would be caught in a lapse of time. They would never have a chance to grow old, entrapped forever in a time warp of infinity. The dimension we call eternity would be their home.

The fantasy of that movie is not so farfetched. In his theory of relativity, Einstein recognized this world of eternity and called it "anti-matter." Could that strange dimension also be the same spirit world described by patients who have had out-of-the-body, after-death experiences? If we have discovered that it is possible to enter timelessness at the speed of light, is this how we enter eternity at death? Are there other ways to enter this world? John 14:2 states that Jesus is working in His Father's "house" now, preparing a place for each of His followers. Isaiah 14:13 refers to the location of heaven as "in the recesses of the north." If heaven is a real place, in existence right now, how could we be transported there? At present we can achieve a speed of 5 miles per second to escape earth's gravitational pull and shoot out into space. But we've never even begun to approach the speed of light, 186,000 miles per second. Even at that speed, it has been estimated that it would take 100,000 years to cross from one end of the Milky Way to the other. So how is anyone ever going to reach heaven?

It occurred to me one day that a story about Philip the evangelist may give us insight (see Acts 8:39). One moment he was baptizing an Ethiopian in a body of water near Gaza, and the next he was "snatched away," finding himself in Azotus, a city along the Mediterranean coast. Patients who have left their body and returned claim to have experienced what may have been similar transportation from one point to another (as recorded in my first book) traveling not at the speed of light, but at the "speed of thought." God's ways are beyond our conception. At least Christians don't have to worry about how we'll get to heaven. Jesus will come to get us when He's finished preparing our new home (see John 14:3).

Believing the Bad

If we believe that the spirit world is real and contains the forces of good and evil, why is it that most of us are intrigued by nightmarish and lurid evil forces but not by angelic beings? In the last few decades we have seen a trend of attraction to evil. The occultic arts of magic, astrology, sorcery, and witchcraft have flourished to the greatest degree since the witch hunts of the seventeenth century.

Courses in parapsychology are increasingly available and popular in some universities. These courses deal with extrasensory perception (ESP), telepathy, ghosts and goblins, UFOs, Ouija boards, Tarot cards, fortune-telling, the ancient Chinese art of *I Ching*, the study of human thought control in Pyramid Power, spiritists, mediums, seances, necromancy, object reading, astral travel, drug trips, psychokinetics, divination, psychic awareness, faith healing, and exorcism. Professors may discuss the occult from a humanist view and try to discard the concepts of God, Satan, heaven, and hell. Biblical studies focus on the Bible's historical and literary significance alone.

Interest in parapsychology and the occultic arts is, of course, not limited to students. A Gallup poll in February 1978 revealed that forty-six percent of the general population believed in ESP and twenty-four percent in clairvoyance (the ability to see things not in sight).

Sixty-two percent claimed to believe in life after death. Fifty-four percent of these same people believed in angels but only thirty-nine percent in devils.[1] Obviously, most people are fascinated with satanic practices but don't want to admit that Satan exists or to call their metaphysical dabblings "evil" or related to "devils."

Doctor Kenneth McAll, a British surgeon and psychiatrist who spent many years in China, is quoted by Billy Graham as saying that there are hundreds of documented cases of individuals who began innocently dabbling in the occult and ended by being either partially controlled or totally possessed by Satan and his demonic hosts.[2]

The same is true in the field of music, with the advent of punk rock and the horrifying saga of Sid Vicious and the Sex Pistols. (After a trail of violence and bizarre behavior, Vicious murdered his girl friend, abruptly ending the group's premiere American tour.) Almost ten years earlier, the Rolling Stones hit number one with their "Sympathy for the Devil." The supposedly unseen is made conveniently visible and audible in theaters and on television and radio. Horoscopes, astrology, palm reading, witchcraft, clairvoyance, and communication with the dead—all totter on a thin edge, a "respectable" separation from actual entry into the realms of Satan.

In Moscow for a heart conference not long ago, I began talking to a Russian doctor who was studying and practicing hypnosis, ESP, and several other types of parapsychology. She described problems she was encountering in some of her psychic communications. These communications were real, she said, not just im-

---

[1]George H. Gallup, *The Gallup Poll, 1978* (Wilmington, Del.: Scholarly Resources, Inc., 1978), pp. 184,185.
[2]Billy Graham, *Angels* (Garden City, N.Y.: Doubleday & Co., 1975), p. 8.

aginary. So fascinating were her experiences that, although she was frightened at times, she didn't want to stop. We maintained correspondence for a time. She wrote of her experimentation with seances and psychic healing. Soon she found herself being controlled by "astral forces." "Spirit guides" entered her private life; even her sleep was interrupted by strange messages. When I last heard from her, her position at the medical institute was under review and her career in jeopardy.

Our society has turned over the mentally ill, the emotionally disturbed, the dying, and the bereaved to the revered profession of psychology. Yet most psychologists are humanists and secularists, uninterested or untrained in spiritual matters. Paul Clayton Vitz, associate professor of psychology at New York University, sums up the problem:

Psychology has become a religion, in particular a form of secular humanism based on worship of the self . . . psychology as religion is deeply anti-Christian. Indeed, it is hostile to most religions. Psychology as religion is extensively supported by schools, universities and social programs financed by taxes collected by millions of Christians . . . [and yet] psychology as a religion has for years been destroying individuals, families and communities.[3]

Vitz goes on to emphasize that, as more and more people discover the emptiness of their self-worship, Christians are presented with a major opportunity to help bring meaning into those individuals' lives.

The Bible acknowledges the existence of evil in the spirit world. But in contrast to our preoccupation with occult and demonic powers, references in the Bible to angels far outnumber references to Satan and his de-

---

[3]Paul C. Vitz, *Psychology as Religion* (Grand Rapids: Wm. B. Eerdman's Publishing Co., 1977), pp. 9,10.

mons. In nearly three hundred places, the Bible speaks of angels being at God's command, beings who are commissioned to aid individuals in their struggles against Satan. Over and over again the Word reminds us that God has already won the battle. Yet how seldom do we remember this! We do our own thing, forgetting that "our struggle is not against flesh and blood, but against the rulers, against the powers, against the world forces of this darkness, against the spiritual forces of wickedness in the heavenly places" (Eph. 6:12).

Although demonic activity and Satan worship are on the increase in the world, the angels are nearer than we think. God says He has given ". . . His angels charge concerning you,/To guard you in all your ways./They will bear you up in their hands,/Lest you strike your foot against a stone" (Ps. 91:11,12).

Angels

Has anyone ever seen an angel? One of the utterly amazing accounts in the Bible is about a prophet named Balaam (see Num. 22). Balaam was off to complete an evil mission when his donkey balked and ran off the dirt road three times. Each time Balaam beat the donkey and forced it back onto the path. Eventually the Lord permitted Balaam to see the invisible spirit world. There, standing in the middle of the way with a sword drawn, was an angel. Was this merely a wisp of smoke? Was the sword imaginary? Apparently not. The angel told Balaam that if he had ridden further the angel would have killed him.

The empire of angels, as described in both the Old and New Testaments, is a vast one. When David was allowed to see the angels as they crossed the skies, he marveled:

119

"The chariots of God are myriads, thousands upon thousands . . ." (Ps. 68:17). When God gave His laws to Moses on Mount Sinai, He came from the midst of ten thousand angels (see Deut. 33:2). Staggered by the sight, Moses said, " 'I am full of fear and trembling' " (Heb. 12:21).

Similar statements are made in the New Testament. John told of seeing "ten thousand times ten thousand" angels ministering to the Lamb of God in the throne room of heaven (Rev. 5:11 KJV). According to Paul, in the last times "the Lord Jesus shall be revealed from heaven with His mighty angels" (2 Thess. 1:7). Another writer referred to an "innumerable company of angels" (Heb. 12:22 KJV).

Neither Lot nor Jacob had any difficulty recognizing angels who manifested themselves in physical form (see Gen. 19:1; 32:1,2). Daniel and John also saw angels (see Dan. 10:5–8; Rev. 10:1). At one time, God Himself appeared to Abraham in the form of an angel, accompanied by two other angels (see Gen. 18).

Not all angels are on missions of mercy. King Herod incurred God's displeasure when he accepted the acclaim of the public as if he were a god. "And immediately an angel of the Lord struck him because he did not give God the glory, and he was eaten by worms and died" (Acts 12:23).

In the best-known Old Testament example, the angel of death was appointed to kill all the firstborn males in Egypt. This destroying angel was a minister of God's judgment (see Heb. 11:28). As instructed by God, the Jews sprinkled the blood of a lamb on their doorposts and so were "passed over" (Ex. 12:18–30). The Passover is still celebrated by many Jews today. That historical incident foreshadowed the blood redemption to be accomplished by the sacrifice of Christ, which ended the need for subsequent sacrifices. His death provides eternal redemption for all who believe.

Angels or the Great Deceiver?

Extensive interviews with the dying have been described by Elisabeth Kübler-Ross, Raymond Moody, Karlis Osis, and others. In several of those incidents, people who were not Christians—even avowed non-Christians—claimed to have had heavenly experiences. That finding troubled me considerably for a while. Then, several theologians pointed me to 2 Corinthians 11:14, 15: "And no wonder, for even Satan disguises himself as an angel of light. Therefore it is not surprising if his servants also disguise themselves as servants of righteousness. . . ." In other words, it is possible that those patients were deceived.

As I mulled over that verse of Scripture, a further explanation occurred to me. Those patients report being received initially into a beautiful light-filled realm. There they encountered a "being of light" who reviewed their life before them. Maybe this was only a judgment session. Then they were reunited with loved ones who had died before. But soon, often as they were walking with their families, they encountered a barrier. Their loved ones went on, but when the patients attempted to cross the barrier, they were forced back into their body, back into the world of pain. They were resuscitated.

Upon return to this world, these particular people are frequently disturbed because they were brought back from a place of ecstasy which they naturally interpret as "heaven." In the place they describe, they have only been "interviewed," not finally judged. Yet because it seemed beautiful, they regard the experience as having been in heaven. And since "death" seemed painless, they are not afraid to die again. From that limited experience, they report that everyone will go to heaven—so eat, drink, and be merry. That is far, far from truth as the Bible teaches it. And far different from other reports given by those who had a negative, hell-like experience.

What about the Devil? Has anyone seen him in their death experiences? Does he reside in the spirit world? Contrary to the beliefs of many (and my own expectations), Satan is not described by patients with hell-like experiences as a tall, skinny guy in a red suit with a pitchfork, cloven feet, and horns. In my studies, although half of the three hundred people who returned from death reported negative experiences, hellish in nature, not one of them reported seeing Satan in the form we usually picture him.[4]

Many grotesque beings were described in the places these patients called *hell*, but, with one exception, no figure other than the "being of light" served as a common denominator. In separate incidents, five patients (two of them doctors by profession) reported seeing a human form with a goat's head, which they all identified as Satan. I had never heard of this before, but it so intrigued me that I looked up some history and found that such a figure had indeed been described in the past. In the Dark Ages, it was called a *Baphomet*, a name derived from two Greek words meaning "absorption into wisdom." The word for *wisdom*, in turn, meant knowledge of "the prince of the world," the enemy of Christ.

---

[4]Many people have asked me if I have analyzed the moral quality of patients claiming a heaven or a hell experience, to see if they "deserved" their particular assignment or experience. I have made no such analyses or judgments. But I can say that those who perceived themselves in heaven and those who perceived themselves in hell were not particularly surprised to find themselves where they were.

One source reported that King Philip IV in 1307 accused the Order of Knights Templar of worshiping this Baphomet.[5]

In the nineteenth century, Eliphas Levi called the same figure the *Sabbatical Goat* or *Baphomet of Mendes*, also known as "Satan of the Witches' Sabbath." This goat-man, worshiped in classic times in the city of Mendes in Egypt, was said to copulate with its female devotees (as the Devil did with his witches).

I went back to the Bible and found that several references to "goats" were translated as "devils" or "wickedness" (see 2 Chr. 11:15 [satyr: he-goat]; Matt. 25:32,33). Then I discovered that the name *Lucifer* means "angel of light" and that he is described in the Bible as an angel of unusual beauty. He was, in fact, once referred to as "star of the morning, son of the dawn" (Is. 14:12).

> You had the seal of perfection,
> Full of wisdom and perfect in beauty. . . .
> You were the anointed cherub who covers,
>   and I placed you there.
> You were on the holy mountain of God;
> You walked in the midst of the stones of fire.
> You were blameless in your ways
> From the day you were created,
> Until unrighteousness was found in you. . . .
> Your heart was lifted up because of your beauty;
> You corrupted your wisdom by reason of your splendor
>   (Ezek. 28:12,14,15,17).

Could such a wonderful creature be what those patients saw when they underwent death? Or did they see an angel of the true and living God? The experience was so vivid, nevertheless, that it resulted in changed lives.

---

[5]Richard Cavendish, *Man, Myth and Magic*, Vol. 2 (New York: Richard Cavendish Corp., 1970), p. 217.

Those with either heaven or hell experiences are never the same again, and surprisingly, what they describe parallels the Bible more than any other religious teaching, regardless of the person's faith.

Without the perfect guide to truth, the Bible, evaluating such experiences is impossible. That guide alone tells the truth about the spirit world and the supernatural.

Battle of the Ages

Like man today, Lucifer took pride in his wisdom and beauty:

> ". . . I will ascend to heaven;
> I will raise my throne above the stars of God,
> And I will sit on the mount of assembly
> In the recesses of the north.
> I will ascend above the heights of the clouds;
> I will make myself like the Most High" (Is. 14:13,14).

Lucifer tried to *be* god and wound up establishing his own kingdom. One third of God's angels followed him (see Rev. 12:4), and warfare between those two kingdoms of good and evil has been taking place since before the beginning of time. Before the earth was created, ". . . God did not spare angels when they sinned [rebelled with Satan], but cast them into hell and committed them to pits of darkness, reserved for judgment" (2 Pet. 2:4).

Thus the two kingdoms of God and Satan, operating in both the spirit world and in the world we see, are locked in what could be called the battle of the ages. That struggle affects our daily lives both in ways in which we are aware and in ways we do not recognize. Satan, the "prince of the power of the air, of the spirit that is now working in the sons of disobedience" (Eph. 2:2) heads up "the world forces of this darkness, . . . the spiritual forces of wickedness in the heavenly places" (Eph. 6:12). He is, for now, the prince of this world. His resources include all the destructive powers of the supernatural. We are told that evidence of those untold powers of the supernatural will become more abundant as the time of the antichrist appears.

This kind of battle between God and Satan had also taken place in the past. For instance, Daniel tells of a vision he had in which he is told of a three-week battle between satanic forces ("the prince of the kingdom of Persia") and angelic forces (Gabriel and Michael) over Persia—modern Iraq and Iran (see Dan. 10).

Do you ever question who will win this battle of the ages? Both forces appear to be powerful. The apostle Paul warned us to keep our spiritual armor on at all times (see Eph. 6:10–18). The apostle Peter admonished us: "Be of sober spirit, be on the alert. Your adversary, the devil, prowls about like a roaring lion, seeking someone to devour" (1 Pet. 5:8).

God will win in the end. We don't need a horoscope or a fortune-teller or a psychic forecast. Revelation 20:10 states: "And the devil who deceived them was thrown into the lake of fire and brimstone . . . and will be tormented day and night forever and ever."

Do you want to be on the winning side? With Christ as your Savior you won't lose. The apostle John said, ". . . greater is He who is in you than he who is in the world" (1 John 4:4). Although Satan is capable of many supernatural deeds, he is allowed to act *only* by the will of the all-powerful and all-knowing God (see Jer. 32:17; 1 John 3:20). Why would God permit Satan to exist at all? That is just one of so many things I don't understand—such as why God loves the world. But His Word assures me of two truths, among others: first, " 'My thoughts are not your thoughts,/Neither are your ways My ways,' declares the LORD" (Is. 55:8). And second, God's ways are right and just (see Ps. 89:14).

The Supernatural and You

You say you still don't believe in the realm of the unseen? Sure you do! You believe in atoms and ions, things you've never seen and never will. You believe in the theories of relativity, the laws of the universe, pulsars, quasars, black holes—things people would have considered ridiculous a few years ago. You also believe in the macabre. You're afraid of the dark after seeing horror shows because you believe what they communicate: There is something supernatural out there. Every time you say "good luck" or cross your fingers—or pray—you give assent to your belief in the unseen world.

Most people believe in prayer, whether they admit it or not. Have you ever thought, "God, help me!" in impending danger? Were you praying to Brahma or Shiva or Vishnu or Krishna or Buddha? Was the exclamation only a figure of speech? Or were you really praying for help from the one and only God?

One afternoon I was flying back home to Chattanooga from a vacation in Daytona Beach. On that trip, Doris and Marvin Thacker were in the plane with my wife Martha and myself. We had to fly lower and lower to stay out of dark, low-hanging clouds. We wished we had filed an instrument flight plan. We knew we had dropped too low when it started to rain all around us. The downpour soon was so heavy that it seeped through the edges of the windshield. I called Jacksonville Center to file an instrument flight plan for a higher altitude. They said they were "too busy" to take our request.

By the time we declared an emergency, the clouds had driven us too low to receive Jacksonville's transmissions. They may have heard us, but we couldn't hear them. We found ourselves flying just above the beach and gradually being blown out over the ocean. We tried to "crab" the plane on a northern track and not lose sight of the beach. If we had tried to land at that time, the heavy waves would have dashed us to bits.

There were only a few options. We could violate regulations and go up into the storm without clearance, risking a violent storm cell or encountering other aircraft, or we could turn back. But by that time we were fifteen minutes into the rainstorm, and I thought we might soon fly out the other side.

In the meantime we had turned slightly inland, flying along a freeway that paralleled the coast. To maintain visibility, we flew barely above the power lines. I was looking for stretches of freeway clear of traffic and suitable for an emergency landing.

Suddenly I heard myself repeatedly saying, "God, help me." The others heard me. I was asking for God's assistance, because I could find no simple solution on my own.

Perhaps you too have faced a dangerous situation and lived to tell about it. Did you also ask for God's help? Of all the gods worshiped today, which one did you call upon? Why not go directly to the true and living God?

I am sure that it was God who helped me. As I was about to land on the freeway, my prayers were interrupted by Martha's shouting "I see a runway! I see a runway!"

Banking the plane sharply in the driving rain, without bothering to contact the tower, I landed on the first runway I could see. We had no idea where we were until Martha read aloud from a large sign near the hangar:

WELCOME TO SAINT AUGUSTINE. I am convinced to this day that God intervened. He answered my prayers.

Psychic Predictions or the Prophets?

As the time of the end draws near, the forces of evil are on the increase. They seem to be getting the upper hand. Man's time on earth seems to be running out, as predicted in Matthew 24, with pollution, starvation, overpopulation, moral degeneration, religious bankruptcy, and the threat of nuclear self-destruction.

Jesus prophesied that there will be " 'wars and disturbances'. . . . 'Nation will rise against nation, and kingdom against kingdom, and there will be great earthquakes, and in various places plagues and famines; and there will be terrors and great signs from heaven' " (Luke 21:9–11). Satan will wage war in the last days, making a last stand, but then losing decisively to God and His angels (see Rev. 20:7–10).

How are human beings preparing for such events? How are we responding as we see our future unfold? Well, a lot of us are doing strange things. As Billy Graham puts it:

Since the beginning of time, man has been interested in what lies beyond the short span of life. Modern man is turning to the occult, Eastern mysticism, palm readers and every other kind of help available to tell [him] about the future. Strangely, only a minority turn to the Bible, the only book that accurately tells the future. The Bible teaches that Jesus Christ is coming back again with His holy angels.[6]

What does the future hold? Should we consult occultic sources? Which psychics would you believe? Should we

---

[6]Graham, p. 136.

believe God's prophets, as recorded in the Bible, or Satan's psychics, who currently vie for headlines in grocery store tabloids?

Time has always proved the Bible's prophets to be unerringly correct. Think for a minute. More than three hundred Old Testament prophecies were fulfilled with the appearance of Jesus Christ; these were made hundreds of years before the events occurred, by many individuals who never had heard of each other. Even small details were accurately predicted. Dozens of prophecies concerning the future of cities, nations, kingdoms, and dynasties have come true exactly as predicted.

The Bible has also made numerous predictions about the time yet to come. The Scriptures state:

- Jesus Christ will personally return to earth to judge the living and the dead.
- Those who belong to Christ will be given new bodies like His own.
- Believers in Jesus Christ will reign with Him for all eternity in His kingdom, which shall have no end.
- Satan and all his forces will be cast aside forever, thrown into the lake of fire.
- A city of God, a palace of gold and precious stones, will be our abode forever.
- The Lord Jesus Christ, together with the Father and the Holy Spirit, will banish forever all death, sorrow, and evil.

Each of us makes a choice. Which type of forecasters should you believe? God's prophets had to be one hundred percent correct under the threat of death (see Deut. 18:20–22). No modern psychic would dare submit to such a test. *All* have made erroneous predictions, despite satanic assistance. Prophecy fulfilled is God's "autograph" on the Bible. Prophecy fulfilled sets it apart from all other "bibles" in the world.

There have always been people who turned to mediums or spiritists, in spite of specific instructions from God: " ' "As for the person who turns to mediums and to spiritists, to play the harlot after them, I will also set My face against that person and will cut him off from among his people" ' " (Lev. 20:6). Oblivious to those warnings, TV talk shows constantly feature psychics with their latest predictions.

I recall some of the forecasts from the past: War with China was predicted in 1968. Walter Reuther was to run for President in 1964. Castro was to be ousted from Cuba in 1970. Nixon would not resign, etc. You, too, can probably recall those goofs. You also may be able to name some current predictions for the future: plane crashes, assassinations, wars, even domestic troubles. So what's new? It makes good copy for cheap tabloid gossip. Remember, some of those predictions will be correct. Guessing alone scores twenty percent. And some psychics' predictions fare much better than guessing. Satan's power is real.

The coming of Jesus Christ is the world's most important fulfilled prophecy. The good news declared in the Bible is that in Jesus Christ our future is secure. He has freed you and me from the uncertainties of fate, from karma and kismet, from sin and guilt. He offers each of us eternal life. Do we believe Him?

Chapter 7

TRUTH OR CONSEQUENCE

I gained a new sense of the tremendous enticements of reincarnation and how it enthralls people, great and small, when I met Raymond Golabiewski. Now the president or board member of several industrial and manufacturing firms in Toronto, Canada, but originally from Jersey City, Raymond grew up determined to be a success. To do that, he decided, a person has to use his brain. When he discovered that the average person uses only about fifteen percent of his brain's capacity, he set about to develop the rest of his brain. One night in Toronto he told me a fascinating story linking reincarnation with the metaphysical world of the occult.

To improve his mind as a businessman, Raymond took some progressive steps. He began by enrolling in the Planned Happiness Institute, where he studied thought transference and astral projection. These practices were nothing more than self-hypnosis, he soon discovered. Entering a trance (called a "somnambulistic state"), he was taught how to create objects in his own mind and attempted to imagine matter into existence by force of will.

Raymond's mind development program led him next to a group who practiced the Science of Being. That group attempted to develop full consciousness in the individual by the regular practice of another form of self-hypnosis called Transcendental Meditation. As his material guide, Raymond used a book by Maharishi Mahesh Yogi entitled *Transcendental Meditation*. He remembered the part that stated ". . . the individual mind should be capable of doing what it likes and be able to materialize its desires without encountering any difficulties or obstacles."[1]

A Christian by family tradition, Raymond said he was completely unaware that hypnosis, or "imaginations," were unacceptable to the Christian faith. He later discovered the following passage (which he recalled for me) which instructed Christians specifically to cast down imaginations: "Casting down imaginations, and every high thing that exalteth itself against the knowledge of God, and bringing into captivity every thought to the obedience of Christ" (2 Cor. 10:5 KJV). Much later Raymond also came to realize that he was accepting humanistic doctrines of meditation which were contrary to God's will: "And be not conformed to this world: but be ye transformed by the renewing of your mind, that ye may prove what is that good, and acceptable, and perfect, will of God" (Rom. 12:2 KJV).

Raymond was taught progressively and cleverly how to use his imagination not only to control himself but for the control of other people. The techniques seemed to be working. To find happiness, he was instructed to think of three interesting things: women, possessions, and self-fulfillment. As he began to master the technique, Ray thought he could project his own mind onto other people by concentrating intently on that specific individual. After getting to know their thoughts, he could impose his

---

[1] Maharishi Mahesh Yogi, *Transcendental Meditation* (New York: Signet Books, New American Library, 1968), p. 229.

own thoughts gradually on that person without his knowing it.

Raymond eventually realized he was actually in league with Satan. But his psychic experiences were fascinating. Satan and Raymond were allies for twenty-five years, as he repeatedly delved into the fields of the supernatural, metaphysics, and parapsychology.

He started experimentation with astrology, a metaphysical game developed by the Babylonians more than five thousand years ago. He began to consult his daily horoscope to determine what to wear and what business decisions to make. To have his horoscope analyzed initially cost only twenty-five dollars, but when the price gradually increased to one hundred dollars, Ray decided to save money and do his own horoscopes.

In his studies he found that astrology, the oldest recorded religion in the world, was based on a belief that the planetary bodies have some sort of superior consciousness that permits them to impel or compel people's affairs on earth. Then Raymond started thinking: *Suppose Christ Himself put the planets where they are; why not ask Him what job to seek, whom to marry, what clothes to put on? Besides, hadn't Copernicus dashed that earthbound view of the universe?*

Reasoning further, Raymond began asking himself: *If astrology is an exact science as it claims to be, then why didn't it foretell the Babylonians (the ones who invented it) the fate that awaited them? Why didn't it forecast a horoscope to enable them to escape their doom?* Raymond later discovered that the horrible fate of Babylon was forecast in Jeremiah 50:13,15, just a few years before it actually happened:

Because of the wrath of the LORD it [Babylon] shall not be inhabited, but it shall be wholly desolate: everyone that goeth by Babylon shall be astonished, and hiss at all her plagues . . . her walls are thrown down: for it is the vengeance of the LORD: take vengeance upon her; as she hath done, do unto her (KJV).

Since astrology didn't work, Raymond tried yoga. The teaching surrounding the exercises promised many things: Women would lose their wrinkles and appear young; men would become vibrant and irresistible. Not only would he be good-looking, Raymond thought (something he had always wanted to be but never thought he was); he would also experience love, peace, and joy. That was the promise.

To do things up right, Raymond decided to employ a private guru to supervise his exercises. The guru instructed him first to stand on his head twenty minutes morning and night. From there he got a new perspective of the world: Everything was upside down. (When his dog got in the habit of licking his face, Raymond abandoned that form of exercise.)

Raymond later realized that in performing those exercises he had been worshiping (through meditation) a god called Brahma, a god he had never heard of. That certainly was a non-Christian act, a thing forbidden by the Lord (Ray had been brought up to believe in the God of the Bible who said, "Thou shalt have no other gods before Me"). He didn't realize when he was practicing yoga that it was a religious exercise of communion with Hindu gods.

By doing some historical research, Raymond found that yoga was part of the old Eastern faith of Hinduism, which was based on reincarnation and karma. In trying to understand Hinduism, Raymond became concerned about the karmic laws controlling reincarnation. If they were true, perhaps he might come back as a dog; if he came back as a dog and started biting people, he might come back as a tick or a flea to live on some other dog. The cycle seemed endless.

On the other hand, he realized if he became good through many reincarnated lives, he could achieve the great union of his soul (atman) with the universal being (Brahma). This union (nirvana) was something he decided he didn't really want after all. The Vedic scriptures, he learned, indicated that upon entering nirvana he would become nothing more than "another drop" in an ocean of nothingness, a drop indistinguishable from every other drop in that ocean.

Raymond started thinking of alternatives. In the Christian heaven, he reasoned, he would be somebody: an individual maintaining his identity, meeting people he knew. Besides, Raymond had heard that some people were in the process of thousands of reincarnations and still had not obtained nirvana because their works were not good enough. *But then, do you get to the Christian heaven by good works too?* he wondered.

He felt better when he remembered he had heard that you get to heaven as a gift from God. But he couldn't remember the exact verse. A friend helped him out and showed him Ephesians 2:8,9 in the Bible, which said that you couldn't obtain heaven through good works. Faith is said to be a gift from God, lest anyone should boast. Well then, are you saved by faith or saved by works? Raymond was unsure. *Maybe the good works polish things up a bit*, he reasoned.

Other things confused him. The Maharishi had stated in his book that "this ultimate reality, the Being, is absolute and being so, is attributeless and cannot create."[2] When Ray studied the Bible, on the other hand, he found

---

[2]Ibid., p. 50.

in Genesis that God created everything and in the Book of John that nothing exists that He has not made. Such a diversity of religious claims troubled Raymond. If it wasn't created, where did the first piece of matter come from for the "big bang" theory? Suppose, instead, the universe was created and since then has existed much as it is today. Then who created it? Creation seemed to be disowned and discredited by many Hindus, as well as by all secular humanists. But God certainly didn't disclaim it, Raymond discovered in his reading. Jeremiah 10:11 said that the gods who didn't create the heavens would themselves perish.

Dissatisfied with the Eastern version of reincarnation, Raymond turned to Western reincarnation and the psychic studies of the famous Edgar Cayce (see chapter 4). *Were Cayce's "spirit guides" in reality the biblical "familiar spirits"?* Raymond wondered. God called occult practices "an abomination" and ordered the Israelites to punish by death any who were wizards or consulters of familiar spirits (see Lev. 20:27; Deut. 18:10–12). After much reading, Raymond realized that Cayce preferred to believe spirit guides rather than God's Word (cf. 2 Tim. 4:3,4). Cayce even wrote his own version of the story of Jesus. Raymond's disenchantment continued to grow when he learned that the leader of his study group, an astrologer and medium, was also an ordained minister of the gospel.

Unhappy with that turn of events, Raymond was still beset with an obsessive compulsion to improve his mind. The more he looked into other fields of parapsychology, the more he found a subtle thread of reincarnation running through all of them. Yet as he appropriated these new psychic vistas, Ray sensed that other parts of his life were becoming contaminated with the occult and supernatural. He realized that forces of evil were involved, but he thought he couldn't do much about it.

He began drinking more, and his tolerance for Scotch whisky increased proportionately. He was smoking three packs of cigarettes daily. He became afraid of the dark, which seemed to attract evil. He began hearing scratching in the walls and ceilings of rooms he entered. He constantly felt a presence of evil, and he knew he was paying homage to it by continuing his study and practice of parapsychology.

To hide his rising anxiety, Raymond made a bold attempt to face his fear head-on. He raced speed boats in national events to prove he wasn't afraid. He began flying airplanes, deliberately directing them into air pockets and storms. Yet he was unable to escape the grip of terror he had hoped to overcome by direct confrontation. His daring actions only worsened his dilemma.

Ray also found his marriage faltering and his life disintegrating. He was on the verge of divorce. He began drinking more and more; "business lunches" lasted long into the afternoon. Then they became still lengthier, sometimes not concluding until midnight. One night he was so drunk he dropped his steak on the floor. Trying to pick it up, he bungled and kicked it under the chair. Trying to pick it up again, he knocked it under the table. When he finally retrieved it, filthy and cold, he ate it anyway.

In desperation, Raymond practiced advanced yoga. In full lotus position, emulating the statue of Buddha, he assumed the form of a perfect triangle, crossing his legs while in the sitting position, his hands on his knees. That position was supposed to symbolize the three points of the lotus triangle: love, joy, and peace. But instead of finding peace, Ray found further terror. This is the way he described it to me:

I heard voices constantly drumming in my head, saying "Kill her, kill her, kill her!" I knew Satan was talking to me. Those were my instructions! Where was the peace, love, and joy I was supposed to receive? What had gone wrong? Everything had been pleasant when I first started these occultic arts to improve my mind. I didn't know at that time that Satan could masquerade as an angel of light. Now I realized that his voice was commanding me to kill my wife. It was very difficult to resist. I was no longer in control of myself. I was under the control of those voices. I became afraid to go to bed at night. I turned on lights when I went to bed, but even with them on, I had to take several belts of booze to boost my courage enough to close my eyes.

Somewhere in the Bible, I scanned a passage that described Satan as the "prince of the air" and "prince of the world." I related it to the *prana* that reincarnationists talk about—the basic force of nature controlling the mind—because it was now controlling my mind and all my thoughts. I was sick of myself. I was sick of what I had done. But I couldn't stop. I still tried to maintain my image as a big shot in business, but under that veneer I was the most miserable of creatures.

One day in January, 1975, I watched a religious television program at the suggestion of one of my business partners, Jim. Jim asked me if I knew Jesus. I thought he was crazy. I knew he was one of the Full Gospel Businessmen. He asked me if I wanted to renounce Satan and the spirit guides. When I said yes, I began crying—crying for no good reason. I couldn't stop. It was as if a shroud had been suddenly removed from me. I felt tremendously relieved. I was free at last!

My wife thought I had joined another cult. But over the next few days she was amazed to find I didn't want to smoke or drink anymore. Then she knew that something had happened, something miraculous. And she wanted it, too!

Our marriage gradually was put together again. I was no longer afraid of the dark. I found that "even the darkness can be light," and I was happy in both places. I read about other people noticing the same thing, as in Psalm 139:12. Think of it! I was set free.

Don't misunderstand, my wife and I still fight, but now we fight fair. We talk things out. I thank God that we have a new life together.

Encounters with individuals like Raymond Golabiewski inspired me to write this book, not only to compare reincarnation and Christianity but to warn others against attempting any "innocent" admixture of the two—which can lead to problems like his. As you read these lines, the battle of the ages—for lives like Raymond's and your own—still rages fiercely. Perhaps in your life today you have seen evidences of God's victory . . . or of Satan's.

Despite the momentary outcomes of our individual battles, the Bible states emphatically in the concluding chapters of the Book of Revelation that God will win in the end. The forces of Satan and his allies will be completely defeated, confined forever to a penitentiary of fire (see Rev. 20:10).

If God has made it clear that He is the ultimate victor (see Col. 2:15; 1 John 3:8), why would anyone choose to join forces with satanic elements the way Raymond did? Why would anyone align himself with a religion that does not have a guaranteed victor? Yet the deception can be great, and the name is reincarnation.

The High Cost of Darkness

Let's consider those questions separately. First, why do false religions (like those that teach reincarnation) continue to flourish—especially in view of the prophetic accuracy of the Bible? I see three possible answers. Followers of false religions either:

—don't know what the Scriptures say,

—or they have read the Bible and choose not to believe,

—or they don't want to read it because they're afraid they might find out what it says.

As the apostle John said, without Christ people love darkness and hate light (see John 3:19,20). They don't believe the gospel of Jesus Christ because they don't *want* to believe it. They would rather live in darkness and enjoy the transient pleasures of sin.

Today even some Christians are allowing themselves to be seduced by such man-made religions as reincarnation, based on concepts that appeal to our human nature. The apostle Paul warned us about these religions long ago: "But the Spirit explicitly says that in later times some will fall away from the faith, paying attention to deceitful spirits and doctrines of demons" (1 Tim. 4:1).

Unhappiness is the only outcome when God is not in control of our lives. Do men and women think they will be happy if they can play God? Does the thrill of sin serve as an escape from spiritual commitment? Does Satan have power to seduce his subjects? We doctors are exposed to some of the most hopeless people in the world: those who have bought Satan's lies. Their miseries are manifested in all kinds of symptoms.

These people live with all sorts of psychosomatic illnesses. They eat too much or too little, are desperately worried or depressed, or feel dejected or overcome by guilt. Unable to recognize the real source of their problems, some become hysterical, some suicidal, and some psychotic. Once astray, they forget that they can look to God for help. Consider the following story.

Dorothy had entered the hospital complaining of irregular heartbeat, nausea, and weight loss. At eighty pounds, she appeared cachectic. The story unfolded that her husband was a trucker and a solid rounder, a lecherous gigolo who used his CB radio to make his introductions to private vehicles with lady drivers. Each trip out he began to spend more and more time away from home.

At first only suspicious, Dorothy finally became convinced of Bob's infidelity. Instead of the traditional overeating to camouflage her insecurity, she started vomiting and retching, rejecting her food because of a nauseating situation which would not disappear. Her laboratory tests in the hospital revealed nothing abnormal, and there were no physical evidences of any disease that would account for her weight loss. This was her third hospitalization with the same complaints. It was her pattern of reaction.

After much thought, she seriously asked herself one day: Should she kill herself, kill her husband, or kill the current other woman? She decided, instead, to separate from her husband.

And that's when Bob started getting sick. Their problem today is self-perpetuating. I'm waiting to see what will happen next, and to whom. Will Dorothy be sick, or will Bob?

Most patients nowadays have a combination of physical and emotional illnesses. It has been estimated that eighty percent of the patients in the average doctor's office today suffer from psychosomatic illnesses, or that it forms a large component of their problems. The frightening thing is that these psychosomatic illnesses can progress to neuroses, to psychoses, or can even lead to suicide.

All of us come in touch with strange people. In one instance I found myself in an unusual debate with a taxi driver, as he drove me to the studio for the "A.M. Los Angeles Show" on KABC–TV.

"You know why I'm just a taxi driver today?" he said. "It's because I mistreated people in my previous life! I used to be a banker before this life, a very successful banker! I especially enjoyed foreclosing loans on poor people. When they couldn't make the payments on their houses and cars, I'd repossess them. I was living in New York at that time, the time when the Empire State Building was just being built. My wife's name was Margaret and we had three sons. I remember every detail about it. I even remember the street we used to live on!

"I was somebody important in that life. In my present life I have a daughter who was born spastic. And do you know why? It's because of her own karma—she has to be paying the penalty for something she did in a previous life of her own. There's no way out for her in this life. That's why you doctors can't do her any good!"

Rationalizing his predicament, this taxi driver could live with it. Just how close he might be to the brink of despair is anyone's guess. He was bitter toward the world. Without his "logical" explanation, life was an unsolvable predicament for him. He refused to seek medical help or to look to God for even a small miracle. Least of all would he consider salvation from his concepts of karma.

I came away from that encounter both compassionate and angry. As a Christian, I longed for him to seek the Savior. To me it was so logical that there was a way out, a solution for his future. Why couldn't he see it? Why would he choose a faith with nothing to offer? *He seems trapped in a losing cause which has no hope.* No one can be brought from such darkness except by the grace of God and the power of the Holy Spirit. The taxi driver may still be brought in from the darkness. At least, that is my prayer.

What Will Happen to Reincarnation?

Allow me a bit of poetic license to conjecture about the future. I foresee reincarnation as a cornerstone for a "new world religion." As I have traveled, visiting all kinds of churches from scientism to satanism, I have seen the embryo of a huge, blended faith which I believe is the Babylon of biblical prophecy. Many other investigators have come to similar conclusions, among them Phillip J. Swihart. He states:

> In my opinion, we will see an increasing drift toward a world religion which will be occult in nature. Such a religion will contain elements of Christianity, Judaism and perhaps Islam, but will have at its base Eastern mysticism. As Christians find themselves an increasingly smaller minority, they will experience greater and greater pressure to become less "narrow-minded" and "bigoted" and become more open to this more "sophisticated faith" which, we will be told, is the apex of all previous religious systems. I believe that this occult world faith will appear to have validity because it will be accompanied by startling supernatural "signs and wonders" (Mark 13:22). It will be hard, even for Christians, not to become part of such a system or at least to seek accommodation with it.[3]

The more I researched, the more I was amazed by the number of predictions of this future world religion. Historically in Scripture, Babylon is a specific geographical location. But prophetically Babylon is not only a place, but also a religion. Many theologians tell me that *Babylon* refers to the universal faith which God has denounced as "an abomination" in the following unusual phrases:

---

[3]Phillip J. Swihart, *The Edge of Death* (Downers Grove, Ill: Inter-Varsity Press, 1978), p. 81.

a mystery,
BABYLON THE GREAT,
THE MOTHER OF HARLOTS
AND OF THE ABOMINATIONS OF THE EARTH
(Rev. 17:5).

The country of Babylon, with its capital city of the same name, was located in what is now known as Iraq. It existed long before Abraham, the father of the Jewish nation, was born. In some Scriptures, Babylon seems to be identified with the Chaldean area (see Is. 13:17–20). In Jeremiah 50 and 51, God mandated that this Babylon would be utterly destroyed in just one day. Sure enough, Babylon was destroyed and has been inhabited only by nomads to this day.

The Babylon of end times is thought by some to represent either the city of Rome as the future world capital, or the future world religion of the Antichrist. I am inclined to believe the latter: Babylon is the apostate church or "world church," a religion that will blend all faiths together (except the true faith), worshiping through different names a god molded into man's image.

Several well-known Bible commentaries have also come to this conclusion.[4] The Wycliffe Bible Commentary gives a further and more precise definition of Babylon:

> . . . I think the closest we can come to an identification is to understand this harlot as symbolic of a vast spiritual power arising at the end of the age, which enters into a league with the world and compromises with world forces. Instead of being spiritually true, she is spiritually false, and thus exercises an evil influence in the name of religion.[5]

---

[4]Jamieson, Fawcett & Brown, *Commentary on the Whole Bible* (Grand Rapids: Zondervan Publishing House, 1961), p. 1578.
[5]Charles F. Pfeiffer and Everett F. Harrison, *The Wycliffe Bible Commentary* (Chicago: Moody Press, 1962), p. 1517.

Most people have heard how the end times will be heralded by earthquakes, pestilence, and wars. But listen to what the apostle Paul also predicts:

For the time will come when they will not endure sound doctrine; but wanting to have their ears tickled, they will accumulate for themselves teachers in accordance to their own desires; and will turn away their ears from the truth, and will turn aside to myths (2 Tim. 4:3,4).

Paul prophesied that even when people have the truth around them, they will not want to listen to it. Does that situation sound familiar? Does it echo daily newspaper accounts? Does it describe some of your friends and associates?

. . . in the last days difficult times will come. For men will be lovers of self, lovers of money, boastful, arrogant, revilers, disobedient to parents, ungrateful, unholy, unloving, irreconcilable, malicious gossips, without self-control, brutal, haters of good, treacherous, reckless, conceited, lovers of pleasure rather than lovers of God; holding to a form of godliness, although they have denied its power. . . . evil men and impostors will proceed from bad to worse, deceiving and being deceived (2 Tim. 3:1–5,13).

Babylon isn't coming. It's here. Babylon, the religion predicted for the end times, is already being practiced by many.

God's Final Word

What will happen to Christians during the end times? What will happen to the rest of the world? The biblical answer is *catastrophe*. The angels of God will break the seven seals of the scroll, blow the seven trumpets, and empty the seven bowls of wrath upon the earth (see Rev. 5–6). Nothing will ever be the same again.

At the climax of that worldwide chaos, everyone of us, living or dead, believer and nonbeliever alike, will have to bow and confess Jesus as Lord. Sooner or later, "at the name of Jesus every knee [will] bow, of those who are in heaven, and on earth, and under the earth, and . . . every tongue [will] confess that Jesus Christ is Lord, to the glory of God the Father" (Phil. 2:10,11).

The God of wonderful love is also a God of terrible wrath in the face of evil. I can imagine His whole countenance changing when He tells us the consequences of walking after other gods: "And it shall come about if you ever forget the LORD your God, and go after other gods and serve them and worship them, I testify against you today that you shall surely perish" (Deut. 8:19).

Our daily newspapers have made horoscopes and astrology so commonplace that we feel immune to them. But God calls those things damnable. Why even glance at something that God so detests? If astrology couldn't help the Babylonians, the inventors of stargazing, to prognosticate their own downfall, how can it be considered reliable for anyone else? God pointed this out when He spoke to the Babylonians through the prophet Isaiah:

> . . . Let now the astrologers,
> Those who prophesy by the stars,
> Those who predict by the new moons,
> Stand up and save you from what will
> come upon you.
> Behold, they have become like stubble,
> Fire burns them;
> They cannot deliver themselves from
> the power of the flame (Is. 47:13,14).

Chapter 8

CAN CHRISTIANS BELIEVE IN REINCARNATION?

Today, some Christians are embracing reincarnation because, in my opinion, they do not understand that it is in direct opposition to Christianity. Under close questioning, these people exhibit no real "combat knowledge" of what the Bible says about following false doctrines—for whatever fringe benefits. That void of biblical awareness is not being filled by churches and other Christian groups, who seem preoccupied with tightening their battle lines over "what the Bible says." All too often, no one will fight you over what the Bible says like another Christian.

Church leaders, please wake up! Rejuvenate in the hearts of your people the reality of bodily resurrection through Jesus Christ. Reincarnation theory is hostile to Christianity. There is no way for a Christian to believe it without forsaking Christ.

Now is the time for Christians to put away even casual interest in horoscopes; fantasies about "past lives"; experimenting with palm readers, clairvoyants, psychics; participation in yoga classes for "exercise and relaxation." Christianity and other religious practices do not mix. And, as we have stated, the activities listed above *are* religious practices. Contrary to the humanly appealing idea of the unification of all faiths, God has said that no such union is possible.

Only One Name

In chapter 5, I outlined the beliefs of reincarnation and Christianity on five major issues. Let's look at those issues a little further. Remember, reincarnation says there is no sin, no hell, no forgiveness required. But you still reap what you sow, in a sense. Because you have not achieved nirvana, you must live another life, and then another, because of your karma.

Christianity acknowledges the existence of sin and evil. But there is a way to avoid judgment. "And there is salvation in no one else; for there is no other name under heaven that has been given among men, by which we must be saved" (Acts 4:12).

What name?

Jesus Christ!

There is no room for reincarnation, Buddhism, Hinduism, parapsychology, or spirit guides. Jesus Christ said, "I am *the* way, and *the* truth, and *the* life; *no one comes to the Father, but through Me*" (John 14:6, italics mine). He also said, "He who believes in the Son has eternal life; but he who does not obey the Son shall not see life . . ." (John 3:36).

Luke, a physician (which makes me feel good), has recorded what Jesus told us about the God to worship and to hold in fearful reverence: "And I say to you, My friends, do not be afraid of those who kill the body, and after that have no more that they can do. But I will warn you whom to fear: fear the One who after He has killed has authority to cast into hell; yes, I tell you, fear Him! (Luke 12:4,5).

The idea that there is no judgment or hell has always been appealing. Except when people get angry and the words *hell* and *damn* are convenient, we almost never hear the subject mentioned in conversations today. "I just can't believe a God of love would judge anyone" is a common argument. "How could a loving God send anybody to hell?"

Wouldn't you love to be able to do your own thing and be accountable to no one? Well, suppose there were no accountability in the world. Take sports, for example. Suppose there were no umpires in baseball to judge the balls and strikes, no basketball referees to call the fouls, no football officials to signal penalties. Without those judgment calls there would be mass confusion. You could never complete a game.

Imagine a nation where all law courts were abolished and criminals were allowed to run free, without ever being brought to justice. When judgment is removed, people degenerate. When there is no accountability, people do their own thing.

Modern writers realize this: take William Golding's *Lord of the Flies*, for example. In that frightening parable, a group of English schoolboys are the sole survivors of a plane crash. Isolated from adults, they try to set up a workable "society." Their life on that island, however, quickly degenerates into warring factions and destruction, when some boys rebel against having rules or principles that all must obey.

Whenever law and order are removed or rebelled against, as when disasters strike in the form of floods, earthquakes, bombings, or blackouts, anarchy soon reigns—with looting, stealing, rape, riots, murder. Doesn't that demonstrate the basic nature of humanity? Without accountability, we are basically evil. We see support for that fact every day in the newspapers. Yet reincarnationists regard each of us as basically good, capable of attaining perfection through our own power.

Courts have been established to judge and sentence law breakers. Yet even with some semblance of judgment and control, we have ample problems. Does the God who made us have no less right to control and judge us?

It is convenient to "forget" that God will not let you and me worship any other gods. God is a God of love, and He jealously guards and protects His own. He knows we cannot be saved through any name but His Son's: Jesus Christ.

To Live Again

The Bible tells us that the destiny of the Christian at death is not to be reborn cyclically, but to enter immediately into God's presence. Paul wrote:

For to me, to live is Christ, and to die is gain [not reincarnation] . . . But I am hard-pressed from both directions, having the desire to depart and be with Christ, for that is very much better; yet to remain on in the flesh is more necessary for your sake (Phil. 1:21,23,24).

In another epistle Paul referred to being absent from the body *and* at home with the Lord (see 2 Cor. 5:8).

In Luke 16 Jesus referred to Abraham as still living spiritually and in the same recognizable form. Jesus also rebuked the Sadducees in Mark 12:27 when He said, " 'He is not the God of the dead, but of the *living*. . .' " (italics mine).

Reincarnation theory attacks God's promise of the *immediacy* of the believer's reunion with God at death. The spirit does not return in another body. It returns to God. "Then the dust [body] will return to the earth as it was, and the spirit will return to God who gave it" (Eccl. 12:7).

Thus, biblical faith teaches that human beings pass from this life into the presence of God. Hebrews 9:27,28 states this clearly: "And inasmuch as it is appointed for men to die once and after this comes judgment, so Christ also, having been offered once to bear the sins of many, shall appear a second time for salvation without reference to sin, to those who eagerly await Him."

The next great event is the judgment, based on the payment for our sins by Jesus Christ on the cross. We cannot atone for our own sins in this life, another life, or in a thousand lives. There is no need for reincarnation in Christianity. Biblical accounts reveal judgment on a specific day, not on a life-to-life basis, as implied by the law of karma. We are told in Acts 17:31 that God " '. . .has fixed a day in which He will judge the world in righteousness through a Man whom He has appointed, having furnished proof to all men by raising Him from the dead.' "

Resurrection or reincarnation? Christ's resurrection is proof to all humankind that we shall all be raised again in body and spirit. Jesus Christ was not reincarnated into someone else's body but returned from death in the same recognizable body He had dwelt in before death. He appeared to people for forty days after the Resurrection. People recognized Him. He talked. He ate. He cooked breakfast. He could be touched. Thomas was amazed when Jesus insisted: " 'Reach here your finger, and see My hands; and reach here your hand, and put it into My side; and be not unbelieving, but believing' " (John 20:27). This Jesus Christ was no ethereal spirit. He said, ". . . touch Me and see, for a spirit does not have flesh and bones as you see that I have" (Luke 24:39).

In anticipation of his own resurrection, King David wrote long before Christ, "I will be satisfied with thy likeness when I awake" (Ps. 17:15). In the New Testament, John assured us that we would be resurrected just like Christ: ". . . it has not appeared as yet what we shall be. We know that, when He appears, we shall be like Him, because we shall see Him just as He is" (1 John 3:2).

The examples go on and on. Christ said to the thief on the cross next to Him: " 'Truly I say to you, *today* you shall be with Me in Paradise' " (Luke 23:43, italics mine). Stephen, as he was stoned to death, looked up into heaven and said, " 'Lord Jesus, receive my spirit!' " (Acts 7:59). Nowhere is reincarnation implied. In another world we will recognize others we have known, but they won't be in someone else's body.

In summary, we see that either the Bible is wrong and reincarnation is true, or the Bible is true and reincarnation is false. Either we are slaves to the law of karma or we have available the atonement of Jesus Christ.

When Christ's disciples saw a blind man, they asked, " 'Rabbi, who sinned, this man or his parents, that he should be born blind?' " And Jesus answered, " 'It was neither . . . but it was in order that the works of God might be displayed in him' " (John 9:2,3). That man's blindness was not caused by any sin he committed. Christ said so, directly contradicting any law of karma. Here is a unique example which puts both human frailty and the sovereignty of God in right perspective.

Yet, in spite of all that the Bible says, some people don't want to change. They don't want to be bothered. Some may actually delight in evil. They follow their spirit guides, creatures the Bible calls demons. The consequences of communicating with or yielding to such spirits are severe: ". . . they did not receive the love of the truth so as to be saved. And for this reason God will send upon them a deluding influence so that they might believe what is false, in order that they all may be judged who did not believe the truth, but took pleasure in wickedness" (2 Thess. 2:10–12).

There comes a point where such people really believe the false words of these spirits and their anti-God philosophies. Is there any way out? Yes, there is.

Personal Problems

Christians have the privilege of communicating with God the Father through prayer, because of Jesus Christ, His Son. Christ's sacrifice makes it possible for me to come into the presence of the pure and holy God. Yoga or transcendental meditation leads only to spirits who hate God. Can they solve my problems? No, they don't even want to. They are out to destroy me. How futile, when there is available the One who created me!

Have you ever not been able to forgive yourself? Have you ever done something you thought was right, only to discover how much it hurt someone else (and yourself)?

What is the worst sin a person can commit, the act that would be hardest of all to forgive oneself for? Murder? If you think so, then *I'm* the worst of sinners. Yes, I confess it. The only reason I am revealing a painful secret I would rather forget is because you, too, may have some secret in your life, some horrible deed you cannot forgive yourself for. "I can't come to God," you may be saying. "I'm too ashamed."

The truth is, if I hadn't let Jesus Christ take my guilt, I wouldn't be able to share this episode with you. Come back with me to my office and see how this murder actually happened. Listen with me to the plight of a distraught young woman.

She came to me one day not because of illness, but because she was pregnant. She had become pregnant through an extramarital passion, and her husband, a heart patient of mine, was not aware of her condition. I reasoned that she was suicidal. I thought I was saving her life by destroying the fetus's life. She had been rejected as an abortion candidate by other doctors, possibly because she was a prominent member of the community. I could list more exonerating reasons for my action, but the truth is I committed murder when I deliberately ended that new life developing inside her.

I can also remember many other sins from my past. Some were pleasurable. Some were not. But this one sin seems to stand above them all, crying "Guilty." The incident staggered the equilibrium of my soul.

I tried to rationalize that thousands of abortions are performed weekly. I could not sleep the night the deed was done, nor could I sleep for several nights thereafter. I was convicted by the Holy Spirit, although I didn't realize it at the time. I was able to find release only through prayer to the *Holy God*. I never could have found release through prayer to my unholy self or to dark spirits.

With great relief, I finally remembered what I had heard in church for many years: God promised, "If we confess our sins, He is faithful and righteous to forgive us our sins and to cleanse us from all unrighteousness" (1 John 1:9). Fellow sinner, I don't want judgment. Do you? I don't want any part of the karma of reincarnation. I want forgiveness and mercy. I want the love of Jesus Christ. He is my substitute for sin, my Savior.

Do you want Him to take away your sin? Then ask Him to do that, to be your *only* God. You are so important to Him that He died for *you* before you loved Him. He will personally wash *you* free of all the dirt in your life if you will ask Him, renouncing and turning your back on sin (see Rom. 5:6–10; Heb. 7:25–27). Come to

Him now by faith—not by feelings or mystical experiences.

Perhaps you believe that you have kept some kind of "personal covenant" with God all these years and have done no wrong? Well, God says we all have fallen short (see Rom. 3:23). "If we say that we have no sin, we are deceiving ourselves, and the truth is not in us" (1 John 1:8). God says we deceive ourselves when we claim to be perfect. We are perfect only through Christ.

I don't know your situation, but I always seem to be in trouble. For me, it's a daily battle. After I claimed Jesus Christ as my Savior, He revealed even more. He revealed even more how sinful I am. I stray every day. I need daily forgiveness and daily renewal.

Life Insurance

When you consider the claims of reincarnation, being born again and again, remember that God says you must be born again—but only *once*. And that is when you come to Christ. It is a spiritual rebirth through the Holy Spirit and not a bodily rebirth (see John 3:5,6).

Choose this day whom you will serve (see Josh. 24:15). You cannot serve two masters (see James 4:4). You cannot be a Christian and also believe in reincarnation.

You say you've been a Christian for twenty years or more, and everyone speaks well of you? Then let me ask you a personal question: How Christian do you rate yourself? Are you truly "full of Christ," or are you a lukewarm Christian (see Rev. 3:15)? What have you done with your salvation since you received it? Have you let it stagnate? Have you just "sat on it," or have you, through obedience, allowed it to grow?

Do you think you are above all this elementary exhortation? You say you tithe regularly, keep all the laws, and commit no sin? The Pharisees said that, too. They claimed those very accomplishments, but Christ didn't think much of them. He called them hypocrites. Is that you?

That's exactly what I was, all my churchgoing life. I treated Christ the way I do aspirin: a little bit is good for you, but too much will make you sick. I wanted just enough religion to make me "respectable"—but not too much. The definition of a good citizen in my part of the country is someone who is a church member. So I joined a church. I thought that would make me a Christian, but for years I was hesitant to "come to Christ" personally. I remained a "head" Christian and not a "heart" Christian.

But I knew I was dirty, and I was getting tired of being dirty. Then I read somewhere that you "come as you are." Wow! You don't have to be clean or respectable. You can, in fact, be filthy. You can be a nobody. You can be a criminal. You can be just like me. Whoever, wherever you are, you can also come to Christ right now, just as you are. And the angels of heaven will rejoice.

"What must I do?" the Philippian jailer asked the apostle Paul. Paul gave him a simple answer: " 'Believe in the Lord Jesus, and you shall be saved . . .' " (Acts 16:30,31). The answer today is the same. It is so simple that I always used to stumble over it. The way to eternal life is to believe in the Lord Jesus Christ. You don't have to straighten your life out first. Ask Christ to be Lord, and then He'll straighten out your life. His Holy Spirit will tell you what to do and how to turn from sin.

You no longer need to consider reincarnation or any other faith when you've been promised the resurrection. As for me, I made this simple commitment and prayer. Ask God to help you make it with me now:

Lord Jesus, I believe you are the living Son of God and my only hope of salvation. I come as I am and ask You to forgive my sins, for I am turning from them. Take control of my life and make me part of Your life and Your work. Teach me each day what I should do through prayer and through Your Scriptures.

I ask You, God my Father, to fill me now with Your Holy Spirit and to seal me in Your service until the day of redemption.

I ask these things in Jesus' holy name. Amen.

If you have prayed that prayer with me, you are now free. If you opened the door of your life to Christ, He has *promised* he will come in—regardless of how messed up your house is (see Rev. 3:20).

No matter how much you may have participated in the occult, be assured that you are now a new creature in Christ. You are liberated to lead a new and different life.

Got a life wish? It *will* come true in Christ Jesus.